# The Culture Revolution:

## Transform Organizational Values and Drive Results

# The Culture Revolution:

## Transform Organizational Values and Drive Results

**Theresa Cochran**

ARCHWAY
PUBLISHING

Archway Publishing books may be ordered through booksellers or by contacting:

Archway Publishing
1663 Liberty Drive
Bloomington, IN 47403
www.archwaypublishing.com
844-669-3957

Interior Image Credit: Theresa Cochran

ISBN: 978-1-6657-6137-6 (sc)
ISBN: 978-1-6657-6138-3 (e)

Library of Congress Control Number: 2024912561

Print information available on the last page.

Archway Publishing rev. date: 07/25/2024

# Contents

# Preface

Have you ever wondered why someone would pour their heart and soul into crafting what they believe to be an indispensable guidebook for organizational and leadership success? What motivates the desire to see your organization thrive and become an irresistible magnet for top talent, outshining even your own? And why would one willingly disclose their playbook in a world of fierce competition?

Such questions gnawed at me as I delved into the depths of drafting this guide, a labour of love born from decades of municipal leadership and private consulting. The catalyst? A seemingly unrelated moment while immersed in the drama of "Billions." As the character Axe grappled with the notion of assisting a competitor, his wife's warning echoed in my mind: "You never give away your playbook. Why now?"

No, I am no Axe, and this Guidebook won't bestow untold riches upon you. Instead, it offers a roadmap to something more valuable: the keys to unlocking your organization's greatness. It's a departure from the antiquated mindset where employees merely clock in, check their brains at the door, and trudge through uninspired days. I firmly believe your organization deserves better, and I'm here to help you achieve it.

Drawing upon a quarter-century of diverse experiences, both triumphs and setbacks, I invite you to journey with me from the shadows of command-and-control leadership into the sunny realm of results-driven collaboration. The culture I envision is one where every individual thrives, where rules yield to innovation, and where the pursuit of excellence is relentless.

This Guidebook is more than just a manual; it's a testament to my unwavering commitment to fostering better leadership and organizational practices. As you navigate its pages, I hope that you'll discover not only actionable insights but also inspiration to challenge the status quo and transform your team from followers of rules to champions of results.

So, buckle up and prepare to embark on a transformative odyssey. Together, let's rewrite the playbook and redefine success, one empowered leader at a time.

"Your Champion."
Theresa

# Acknowledgements

I am immensely grateful to my husband, Dave, and my children and their fabulous partners for their unwavering support and patience as I delved into the intricacies of leadership and organizational dynamics. Their willingness to listen and provide feedback to my endless musings on the subject has been a constant source of inspiration.

To my previous leaders who ignited the flame of passion within me and instilled in me the belief that there is always a better way, I owe a debt of gratitude. Among them, Cameron Roberts stands out as a beacon of exemplary leadership, consistently inspiring greatness and fostering a culture of accountability and results-driven action.

I am also indebted to the countless colleagues, many of whom have become cherished friends, who have walked alongside me on this journey. Each interaction and shared experience has contributed to my growth as a leader and has reinforced the importance of modelling the way and holding oneself accountable.

Though there are too many to name individually, they all know their profound impact on shaping my perspective and fueling my passion for results-based leadership. Their collective wisdom and unwavering support have propelled me forward, embodying the essence of results-based accountability and serving as the guiding force behind my vision for a more impactful future.

Lastly, I extend my heartfelt thanks to the authors whose works have served as guiding lights throughout the writing of this book. Their insights and perspectives have enriched my understanding of leadership and accountability, shaping the very essence of the principles I seek to share.

To each and every individual who has contributed to my journey, whether through direct mentorship, collaboration, or the written word, I offer my most profound appreciation. Your collective influence has been instrumental in shaping both this book and my personal and professional growth.

With gratitude,
Theresa

# Introduction

In my mind's eye, I paint a picture of the ideal workplace. In this oasis, inspiration flows freely, motivation is abundant, and encouragement is woven into the very fabric of daily interactions. It's a place where accountability reigns supreme, and leadership is not just a title but a beacon of guidance and empowerment. Sadly, I've also witnessed environments where such qualities are scarce, where disengagement and discontent are the norm—a reality I vehemently reject, and I suspect you do too.

Welcome to the heart of this book: culture. The invisible thread weaves through every aspect of organizational life, shaping attitudes, behaviours, and, ultimately, results. As leaders, the imperative is clear: either we shape our culture, or it shapes us. It's a sentiment echoed in countless boardrooms and management meetings—"Either you manage your culture, or it will manage you." If enduring success and a lineup of top-tier talent vying to join your ranks are your aspirations, then the journey begins with culture.

Doesn't that sound like the organization you want to work for? As I have discovered throughout my career, many employees and leaders wish to experience something different at work. Still, they are unsure how to achieve lasting cultural change. Where do you start?

Of course, it will take considerable time and effort, and there is no "cookie-cutter" approach to transforming your culture. Even so, action committed to transforming your culture from a focus on rules to control behaviour to a focus on accountability for results will align employees to a method of doing business that will improve shareholder value. I must stress and will discuss later that executive commitment and exceptional leadership are imperative to success.

Moreover, transforming your organization from a rules-based to a results-driven approach offers significant benefits. Results-based organizations leverage operational performance data to foster continuous learning and improvement, a practice supported by several principles outlined later in this book. Research indicates that such organizations cultivate a supportive and innovative culture, leading to increased employee satisfaction and organizational commitment. This shift effectively mitigates the negative impact commonly associated with rules-based corporate cultures.

Many organizations use results-based accountability to support their operations, including the Organisation for Economic Co-operation and Development (OECD) and the United Nations, to name the most significant and impactful. These organizations understand that to motivate individuals worldwide in potentially life-threatening circumstances, managing for results is imperative for success.

To guide you on the transformative journey from rules to results, I present the Cultural Transformation Framework—a roadmap to unlocking your organization's full potential. Within its pages lie the keys to fostering a culture where every employee is not just present but fully engaged, accountable, and inspired to reach new heights every day. Imagine a workplace where the pursuit of excellence is not a chore but a joyful pursuit, where success is celebrated, and challenges are met with unwavering determination.

This framework is more than just a collection of strategies; it's a blueprint for crafting a culture that breeds success. Each element is meticulously designed, with clear objectives and actionable tactics that, when embraced, pave the way for profound transformation. Picture a workplace where every individual is empowered to be their best selves, where their contributions are valued and their potential unleashed.

But the benefits extend far beyond mere productivity. By embracing cultural transformation, you're not just enhancing operational efficiency but creating an environment where employees thrive. Imagine a workforce brimming with motivation and satisfaction, where retention rates soar, and talent acquisition becomes effortless. Your people aren't just employees—they're your organizational superpower, propelling your business toward unparalleled success year after year.

So, join me on this exhilarating journey of cultural transformation. Let's unlock the potential within your organization and chart a course toward a future where success isn't just a goal; it's a way of life.

# PART 1

## Cultural Roadblocks: Overcoming Obstacles in Organizational Culture

# Rulebound Realities: Navigating the Pitfalls of Rules-based Organizations

Step into the world of rules-based organizations, and you'll find yourself navigating a landscape marked by hierarchy, command-and-control structures, and a labyrinth of policies dictating behaviour. These organizations are meticulously organized, tightly regulated, and firmly rooted in the status quo—a culture where innovation struggles to thrive and creativity is stifled by fear of deviating from the norm.

# RULES BASED ORGANIZATIONAL CULTURES

1. REGULATION

2. COMMAND & CONTROL LEADERS

3. IN THE BOX THINKING

4. AVOIDANCE / BLAME

5. LACKS DIVERSITY

6. POOR RETENTION

7. NEGATIVE VIBE

8. POOR ORGANIZAITONAL RESULTS

In such environments, employees find themselves confined within the rigid restrictions of policy and procedure, with little room for autonomy or self-expression. The prevailing ethos is compliance, where stepping out of line is met with apprehension and conformity is rewarded over initiative.

Management, too, subscribes to this regulatory approach, seeking to influence results through a maze of rules rather than fostering trust and empowerment. However, the unintended consequence is a workforce that feels constrained, stifled, and disempowered, with leaders burdened by the role of enforcers rather than facilitators of progress.

Rules-based organizations also have high employee turnover and significant organizational silos. Further, as I have witnessed, after countless times employees' great ideas are turned down by their leaders, employees instead "check their brain at the door." Accordingly, rules-based organizations tend to "fall below the line" in Performance and accountability, and employees may often follow the victim cycle described below[1].

There are examples of when command and control leadership may be required, such as in an emergency where the International Control System (ICS) is invoked to ensure all issues are appropriately managed. I have seen the ICS in action and have supported incidents. In these situations, I wholeheartedly support the agreed-upon rules being adopted!

## Unraveling the Dynamics of Victimhood

Have you ever found yourself amidst the chorus of discontent within an organization? Perhaps you've encountered colleagues who incessantly lamented the status quo, bemoaning their inability to effect change and improve their circumstances. While their grievances may hold validity, a pattern emerges when complaints persist without corresponding action—a pattern known as the Victim Cycle.

In this cycle, individuals become entrenched in a mindset of powerlessness, perpetuating a culture of negativity that hampers progress and stifles innovation. Rather than seizing opportunities for growth and transformation, they remain entangled in a cycle of blame, rendering themselves and their organizations immobile.

But the implications extend far beyond mere morale; this cycle poses a tangible threat to achieving results, thwarting the collective potential of individuals and organizations alike. It's a phenomenon as insidious as it is pervasive, capable of undermining even the most well-intentioned efforts toward success. Join me as we explore the depths of the Victim Cycle, its causes, consequences, and—most importantly—strategies for breaking free from its grip.

## Unveiling the Root Causes and Far-Reaching Effects

In the Victim Cycle, employees develop elaborate excuses to ensure no accountability if they are less than successful, ultimately limiting any hope of sustained success in meeting objectives.[2] It is disheartening to witness and is a challenge to manage and change.

Understanding the causes and consequences of certain phenomena is paramount to fostering growth and effecting change in the intricate web of human behaviour and organizational dynamics. Within an organizational culture, recognizing the underlying factors contributing to specific behaviours and their subsequent outcomes is essential for leaders and individuals.

Several contributing factors are at the heart of the Victim Cycle, each perpetuating and reinforcing the other. One prominent cause is a pervasive sense of learned helplessness stemming from repeated experiences of perceived failure or lack of control. Individuals thwarted in their attempts to effect change may become resigned, adopting a passive stance and surrendering agency over their destinies. Moreover, organizational structures and leadership styles prioritizing hierarchy over empowerment can exacerbate feelings of powerlessness, further entrenching individuals in the Victim Cycle. Additionally, a culture of blame and finger-pointing, whether at the individual or organizational level, can fuel a sense of victimhood, perpetuating a cycle of negativity and disempowerment.

Employees regularly showing signs of the Victim Cycle continually "fall below the line in their work."[3] This non-accountability can creep into the organization over time, gradually enough that it is left unnoticed until it is part of the culture, deep-seated and ingrained. Initially, it may feel as if the employee(s) excuses for non-action are reasonable, moving into blame for the why not, and then finally just becoming "the way it is around here," [4] below the iceberg behaviours that erode the culture day after day. For high-performers, "the way it is around here" is the most disheartening, as moving the organization toward action and results is near impossible.

During my tenure at a previous organization, I was immersed in developing a new strategic plan with my team. As we brainstormed ideas and envisioned the possibilities, I approached each member with a simple yet pivotal question: "What would you do next year if budget constraints were no obstacle?"

The responses varied, but one stood out starkly. When I posed the question to a particular employee, their response was met with silence—a telling sign that we were in for a bumpy ride. It soon became apparent that, in this employee's mind, the status quo held far more appeal than the daunting prospect of charting new territory and striving for innovative outcomes.

**THE VICTIM CYCLE**

WHERE WE STAY STUCK

**STEP 1**
IGNORE / DENY THE PROBLEM

**STEP 2**
COVER YOUR TAIL

**STEP 3**
TELL ME WHAT TO DO ATTITUDE

**STEP 4**
FINGER POINTING

**STEP 5**
BLAME SOMEONE ELSE

Undeterred, I persisted in my efforts to inspire change and empower this individual to embrace new challenges. I presented them with opportunities to spearhead projects aligned with their expertise and passions, projects that promised to make a meaningful impact on our community.

However, instead of enthusiasm and eagerness, I was met with a litany of excuses and resistance. From claims of limited resources to apprehensions about potential failure, it was evident that this employee had succumbed to the devious grip of the victim cycle.

At that moment, as I listened to their excuses and observed their reluctance to embrace change, I realized the profound impact of the victim cycle on individual behaviour and organizational progress. It was a sobering reminder of the importance of fostering a culture of accountability and empowerment, where individuals feel empowered to seize opportunities and drive meaningful change, rather than succumbing to a mindset of helplessness and complacency.

This experience served as a poignant lesson in leadership, reinforcing the imperative of identifying and addressing the victim cycle within organizations to cultivate a culture of resilience, innovation, and success. It is easy to slip into the Victim Cycle as we are all human. Yet, it is worth a self-examination to ensure you and your employees are not declining. Look for the next time you tell yourself you would do things differently if it were your company or if you hear the words, "Just tell me what you want me to do, and I'll do it," as these are signs of the Victim Cycle in action.

## The Lasting Consequences

The consequences of the Victim Cycle are far-reaching and multifaceted, exerting a profound impact on individuals, teams, and organizations as a whole. At the individual level, prolonged exposure to a victim mindset can erode self-esteem and confidence, inhibiting personal growth and development. Moreover, individuals trapped in the Victim Cycle often struggle to take ownership of their actions and outcomes, relying instead on external factors or circumstances to dictate their fate. This relinquishment of responsibility can lead to a culture of passivity and apathy, stifling innovation and hindering progress. On a broader scale, organizations afflicted by the Victim Cycle may experience decreased morale, increased turnover, and diminished productivity as individuals and teams become mired in blame and negativity. Ultimately, the consequences of the Victim Cycle extend beyond the confines of the organization, affecting its reputation, competitiveness, and long-term viability.

## Reflection Questions to Drive Organizational Transformation

1. How can organizations transition from being rules-based to fostering a culture that inspires employee motivation and fuels innovation?

2. In what ways do rigid rules and regulations hinder leadership roles and contribute to employee turnover, and how can organizations mitigate these effects?

3. What steps can organizations take to break free from the "Victim Cycle" and unleash their full potential for achieving ambitious goals?

4. How do individuals fall into the trap of the Victim Cycle, and what proactive measures can leaders take to empower employees and drive meaningful change?

5. What strategies can organizations employ to prevent the gradual infiltration of a culture of non-accountability, and what are the enduring consequences of such a culture?

6. Can you share an inspiring example of an organization that successfully overcame the Victim Cycle and transformed into a beacon of accountability and innovation?

7.  What concrete steps can organizations take to break the shackles of the Victim Cycle and cultivate a culture that champions accountability, creativity, and continuous improvement?

# Freeing Performance from the Shackles of Rules

**2**

A spectrum of workplace cultures exists in the maze of corporate structures and organizational hierarchies. At one end, you'll find environments where rules dictate every action and policy reigns supreme. It's a landscape saturated with rigidity, where creativity is stifled, and the fear of stepping out of line looms large.

For many individuals autonomy and trust are the lifeblood of productivity. In environments where rules are shackles, employees crave leaders who empower, motivate, and support them – leaders who listen, understand, and always have their backs.

Yet, far too often, we find ourselves amidst organizations that respond to challenges with the knee-jerk reaction of crafting yet another policy. It's a culture of fear and conformity, perpetuating what I've come to call the 'whack-a-mole organization.' In these environments, employees are discouraged from innovation and change and forced to navigate a labyrinth of rules for fear of public shaming and retribution.

But amidst this sea of conformity, some refuse to be assimilated. Meet June, a bright and ambitious young professional who recently embarked on her journey within one such organization. Excited to make her mark and contribute to the team, June soon discovered a reality she hadn't anticipated.

From the moment she stepped through the doors, June felt the weight of the rules bearing down on her. Every action and decision was scrutinized, leaving little room for creativity or innovation. It wasn't long before June realized she was trapped in a culture of fear—a culture where stepping out of line meant facing public shame and retribution.

However, June was determined not to be confined by this environment's limitations. She questioned the status quo, challenged outdated rules, and refused to accept mediocrity as the norm. Though her colleagues may have called her rebellious, June saw herself as a catalyst for change—a voice advocating for a better way forward.

As June navigated the complexities of this rule-driven culture, she couldn't help but wonder: why did the organization cling so tightly to its policies, even when they stifled innovation and hindered progress? And more importantly, was there a way to break free from this cycle of fear and conformity?

Let's consider some key points to assess where our organizations sit on the continuum from rules to results. From evaluating leadership styles to reflecting on our willingness to challenge the status quo, let's explore how we can advocate for a new paradigm of leadership—one built on trust, empowerment, and a relentless pursuit of excellence.

1.  Evaluate your organization's leadership style and reliance on rules. How does this impact the workplace environment, particularly in stifling creativity and innovation due to a fear of non-conformity?

2.  Reflect on whether your organization creates numerous policies for various issues. How does this proliferation of rules affect progress and employees' willingness to experiment with new approaches?

3.  Assess whether your organizational culture is "fear-based." Do employees seem focused on maintaining the status quo to avoid potential trouble, and how does this affect their willingness to take risks and their overall motivation?

4.  Consider your and your colleagues' willingness to challenge outdated and unproductive rules. Is there a culture of questioning norms and seeking innovative solutions within your organization?

5. Reflect on whether your organization is exploring an alternative leadership approach that prioritizes care, encouragement, motivation, and inspiration over excessive rules. How does this approach impact leadership effectiveness, employee strengths, accountability, and overall organizational results?

6. Recognize the importance of resisting assimilation into a highly regulated culture. How can you advocate for a more empowering, motivating, and trusting leadership style that balances rules with employee empowerment and innovation?

As we conclude this chapter, it's clear that the dichotomy between rule-driven cultures and environments that prioritize empowerment and innovation is stark. We've witnessed the stifling effects of excessive rules and policies, the erosion of creativity and motivation, and the pervasive fear that permeates organizations entrenched in the 'whack-a-mole' culture.

But amidst these challenges lies an opportunity for transformation. The next chapter will spotlight cultural transformation—a journey toward results-driven cultures prioritizing accountability, innovation, and employee engagement. It's a journey that begins with a commitment to challenging the status quo, advocating for empowering leadership styles, and fostering a culture of trust and collaboration.

## Exemplary Organizations: Cultivating a Culture of Empowerment and Innovation

In exploring organizational cultures, it's essential to highlight companies that serve as beacons of inspiration in their commitment to empowerment, innovation, and accountability. These exemplary organizations have forged cultures prioritizing trust, autonomy, and collaboration over rigid rules and policies, resulting in exceptional performance, employee engagement, and organizational success.

1. Netflix: Embracing "Freedom and Responsibility"

At Netflix, the "Freedom and Responsibility" mantra guides the organization's culture. Employees are empowered to make decisions without extensive oversight, fostering a sense of ownership and accountability. By trusting its employees to act in the organization's best interests, Netflix has created a dynamic and agile work environment that drives innovation and success[5].

2.  Google: Fostering Creativity and Innovation

    Google is renowned for its culture of creativity and innovation. The company encourages employees to pursue their passions and explore new ideas through initiatives like the famous "20% time," where employees can dedicate a portion of their workweek to personal projects. This commitment to experimentation and learning has led to groundbreaking innovations that have reshaped industries and changed the way we interact with technology[6].

3.  Zappos: Prioritizing Employee Happiness and Customer Service

    Zappos places a strong emphasis on employee happiness and customer service. CEO Tony Hsieh has cultivated a culture of trust, transparency, and collaboration, empowering employees to take ownership of their roles and deliver exceptional customer service. By prioritizing the well-being of its employees, Zappos has created a loyal and motivated workforce that drives the company's success[7].

4.  Patagonia: Championing Environmental Sustainability and Social Responsibility

    Patagonia is committed to environmental sustainability and social responsibility; its culture reflects these values. The company encourages employees to pursue their passions, supports work-life balance, and prioritizes transparency and open communication. By aligning its organizational values with its employees' values, Patagonia has created a culture of purpose and passion that drives positive impact within and beyond[8].

These exemplary organizations are potent examples of the transformative potential of cultivating a culture of empowerment, innovation, and accountability. By prioritizing trust, autonomy, and collaboration, these companies have unlocked the full potential of their employees, driving innovation, creativity, and success. As we continue our exploration of organizational cultures, let us draw inspiration from these shining examples and strive to build cultures that empower and inspire.

# 3

# Cultural Transformation – A Spotlight on Results

A results-based organization is one where everyone directly or indirectly contributes to achieving results or outcomes intended to impact the community, citizens, or customers positively[9]. Additionally, research suggests that results-based organizations create encouraging and innovative cultures that positively affect employee satisfaction and organizational commitment, reducing the negative impact on employee satisfaction often seen in rules-based corporate cultures[10]. Further, focusing on accountability, with a roadmap to get there, will allow employees to overcome the roadblocks, biases, and excuses that keep the organization stuck in the victim cycle.[11]

A rules-based culture can stifle many organizations' creativity, innovation, and employee empowerment. Such cultures often exhibit risk aversion, conservative management styles, and top-down decision-making processes. However, the good news is that transformation is within reach, especially with strong leadership guiding the way.

By embarking on a cultural transformation journey, organizations can unlock myriad benefits. Increased efficiency and effectiveness, heightened employee satisfaction and motivation, enhanced leadership competency, and a culture of personal and collective accountability are just a few of the outcomes to anticipate. The prospect of such positive changes is indeed enticing.

But how does one transform an organization from a rule-driven environment to one where accountability and innovation thrive? The answer lies in strategic planning and deliberate action. It's about creating a culture where every employee feels personally invested in the organization's success and is empowered to contribute to its growth.

Enter the Cultural Transformation Framework—a comprehensive guide designed to address organizational challenges and facilitate the transition towards a more accountable and innovative culture. This framework outlines specific objectives and tactics to drive cultural change over time. Throughout this book, we'll delve into the framework's components, offering insights and strategies to support your organization's transformational journey.

With dedication, perseverance, and a clear roadmap, the path to a more accountable, innovative, and thriving organizational culture becomes not just feasible but inevitable.

# Summary of Part 1: Transitioning to a Results-Based Organization

In Part 1 of our journey toward organizational transformation, we explored the fundamental differences between rules-based cultures and results-based organizations. We discovered that while rules-based cultures may inhibit creativity and innovation, results-based organizations foster accountability, innovation, and employee empowerment.

We learned that a results-based organization is one where everyone, from leaders to frontline employees, contributes directly or indirectly to achieving positive outcomes for the community, citizens, or customers. Research suggests that such organizations cultivate encouraging and innovative cultures, leading to higher levels of employee satisfaction and organizational commitment.

Moreover, we identified the challenges inherent in rules-based cultures, including risk aversion, conservative management styles, and top-down decision-making processes. However, with strong leadership and a commitment to change, transformation is not only possible but also highly beneficial.

As we move forward, armed with the insights gained in Part 1, we'll delve into the Cultural Transformation Framework—a strategic roadmap designed to guide organizations through the process of cultural change. By implementing the framework's objectives and tactics, we can overcome the roadblocks, biases, and excuses that keep organizations stuck in the victim cycle.

# PART 2
## The Action Plan

# Introducing the Rules to Results – Cultural Transformation Framework

The journey towards organizational transformation requires not only vision and commitment but also a roadmap. This guiding framework illuminates the path forward and empowers leaders and teams to navigate the complexities of cultural change. With this imperative in mind, the Rules to Results—Cultural Transformation Framework was conceived.

The framework originated from the foundational work completed during my MBA Management Project, drawing upon insights gained from extensive research and practical experience. However, its evolution has been shaped and enriched by the collective wisdom of forward-thinking authors and thought leaders whose ideas have inspired and informed its development.

At its core, the Cultural Transformation Framework serves as a comprehensive blueprint—a 'how-to' guide for organizations embarking on the journey from rules-based cultures to results-driven environments. It is not a one-size-fits-all solution but rather a flexible tool that can be tailored and adapted to suit your organization's unique needs and challenges.

As you embark on this transformative journey, remember that change takes time. It requires patience, perseverance, and a steadfast commitment to the end goal. But amidst the inevitable roadblocks and challenges, remember to stay focused, have fun, and keep moving forward.

The Rules to Results - Cultural Transformation Framework is your compass, your guiding light in the tumultuous seas of organizational change.

Embrace it, wield it with intentionality, and watch your organization evolve into a beacon of accountability, innovation, and excellence

## How Clear Is Your Map

Have you ever had a job where you needed clarification on how you aligned or where the organization was going? I am sure many of you said "yes." Accordingly, if you want to promote understanding of where you are going, develop a map. The map (vision) must describe where you are going and how you expect to get there; otherwise, your folks will get lost. The leadership team must guide the way in all aspects and develop, agree upon, and champion the strategy and vision. It is vital to note that you cannot delegate Transformative Cultural change to Human Resources (HR), Organizational Development (OD), or anyone else.

Would you agree that most culture change and employee engagement activities are located in and expected of the HR/OD department to spearhead and achieve? While these roles are essential in the Transformation, the leadership team must maintain ownership of the process and lead the culture change at every level of the organization, ensuring that the change effort is prioritized correctly at the top of every leadership team agenda".[12] Otherwise, the result will be half-hearted as leaders are not accountable for embracing the change entirely as they don't report to HR/OD, and the Cultural change goals tend to be a check-box without action.

The vision must include a clear and concise definition of the culture the organization wants to emulate and actions that will guide the way. A clear map forward provides your employees with clarity of purpose and direction. It simplifies decisions across the organization and helps coordinate all staff's actions quickly and efficiently[13]. All employees should be able to speak to the organization's top objectives and why they matter; however, I bet if you went and chatted with your folks, you would find employees either have different answers or don't have a clue. "If employees don't know where you are going, how can they help you get there?"[14]

What is the risk of no vision, purpose, or reason for existence? As I have witnessed repeatedly, a lack of vision and collective meaning on the part of the leadership will leave you achieving only minimal results with unfocused, uncommitted employees. Further, I must stress that the CAO/CEO must fully support Cultural Transformation to ensure that the leadership team is entirely on board; otherwise, the result will be less than ideal. *I contend this is one of this strategy's most crucial elements.*

In addition to ensuring the leadership is guiding the way, it is essential to

- Articulate a clear vision; how do employees win at their jobs
- Communicate the vision effectively over and over and over
- Align goals with actions always; be diligent

A comprehensive communication and implementation strategy is necessary to identify the critical roles and responsibilities to ensure accountability for results. Leaders must ensure employees have the tools and resources to succeed, and formal and informal incentives are needed to support ongoing alignment and attention to the Transformation.[15] Otherwise, employees will jump off the bus, running into the arms of your local competitors to seek employment.

So, how do you get this vision on paper and employees on the bus? John Kotter[16] (whom I consider a Change Master, like Yoda!) suggests the vision must be:

- *Conceivable:* Be descriptive; express a picture of what the future will look like
- *Enviable*: Appeals to the long-term interests of employees, customers, stakeholders
- *Achievable:* Comprises realistic, attainable goals grounded in a clear and reasonable understanding of the organization (SMART)
- *Focused:* Is clear enough to guide decision-making for all levels of staff
- *Adaptable:* It is generally sufficient for all employees to have a "line of sight" and for possible changing conditions
- *Communicable:* Is easy to communicate; can be successfully explained within five minutes.

As discussed in the book *Contented Cows Still Give Better Milk,* "Once you've made the journey and its purpose impeccably clear... it's time for everyone (no exceptions) to either enthusiastically get in the boat and start rowing or be thrown overboard! There can be no place for half-hearted interest or effort." That sounds quite harsh, and I would never throw anyone overboard. Still, it would be best if you got folks in the right seats, working passionately within their strengths, or after every possibility is exhausted, leaders must urge the folks not on the bus to seek a better fit elsewhere.

## Where is the "Line of Site"

In addition to a strong vision provided by the leadership team, everyone needs to understand the results that you are trying to achieve. The "North Star," if you will. Further, the focus must remain on Results instead of goals as "results imply that either you will or have already achieved something; it is aspirational in nature."[17] Leaders and employees must understand the expected results and have a plan for what will be different. After all, if we remain the same, how can we change? Consequently, it is essential to identify actions and the specific deliverables required to produce the specified results.

It is valuable to note that accountability for results is scary for many employees. I have seen the best employees shy away from quantifiable measures for fear of failure and reprimand. Consequently, when asked to produce goals and outcomes, they tend to be murky to avoid explanations if things go wrong. Additionally, rules-based cultures fail to achieve long-term goals as employees are focused on today's goals instead of the long game. This short-term thinking is dangerous for any business, but this is to the detriment of future generations in government. Consequently, it is essential to create alignment with a clear statement of the results you want to achieve and further consider how you define accountability within your current culture.[18]

## The Happy Techs Corporation: A Journey of Successful Transformation

Consider the following scenario:

At The Happy Techs Corporation, a mid-sized fictitious Tech company, the leadership team grappled with declining employee morale and stagnating innovation. Employees remained disengaged and unmotivated despite their efforts to introduce new initiatives and policies. Recognizing the need for a cultural transformation, the CEO, Sophie, decided to take decisive action.

Sophie gathered her leadership team for a strategic planning retreat to redefine the company's vision and chart a course for the future. After hours of brainstorming and discussion, they emerged with a bold new vision: to become the industry leader in cutting-edge technology solutions, driven by a culture of creativity, collaboration, and continuous improvement.

Excited by the possibilities, Sophie and her team communicated the vision to the rest of the organization. They held town hall meetings, sent company-wide emails, and launched an internal campaign to rally employees around the new vision. These efforts ensured every employee understood the company's direction and felt inspired to contribute to its success.

But crafting a vision was only the first step. Sophie knew they needed to align organizational goals with individual actions to bring the vision to life. They implemented a performance management system that directly linked employee objectives to the company's strategic priorities, ensuring everyone worked towards the same goals.

To further support alignment, Sophie introduced new training programs and incentives to develop employee skills and foster collaboration across teams. She also encouraged open communication channels, where employees could share ideas and feedback to drive innovation and continuous improvement.

Over time, the effects of the cultural transformation became apparent. Employee morale soared as individuals felt empowered to take ownership of their work and contribute meaningfully to the company's success. Innovation flourished as teams collaborated on new projects and initiatives, driving growth and profitability.

Through a clear vision and alignment of goals with actions, Sophie and her leadership team successfully led the organization through a transformative journey, positioning the company as a leader in the industry and ensuring its long-term success.

## Considerations for Leaders

In the fast-paced business world, leaders are often faced with the daunting task of steering their organizations toward success amidst uncertainty and change. Take, for example, the journey of Happy Techs Corporation, grappling with declining morale and stagnating innovation. Recognizing the need for a cultural transformation, CEO Sophie embarked on a bold initiative to redefine the company's vision and align organizational goals with individual actions.

Through effective communication, strategic alignment, and a commitment to fostering collaboration and innovation, Sophie and her leadership team successfully navigated the Happy Techs through a transformative journey. Their experience serves as a testament to the critical role of leadership in driving organizational change and achieving long-term success. As leaders, we can glean valuable insights from their journey, particularly in crafting a clear vision, aligning goals with actions, and fostering accountability for results. Let's examine these factors in more depth.

1. Start by defining a clear and concise vision that outlines where the organization is headed and how it plans to get there. Ensure that the vision is articulated to resonate with employees and give them a sense of purpose and direction.

2. Cultural transformation cannot be delegated solely to HR or OD departments. It requires active leadership involvement at every level of the organization. Leaders must champion the change effort and prioritize cultural transformation on the leadership team's agenda.

3. Communicate the vision repeatedly and consistently to ensure all employees understand where the organization is headed and why. This ongoing communication helps create alignment and ensures everyone works towards the same goals.

4. Align organizational goals with individual actions to ensure everyone is working towards achieving the desired outcomes. Monitor progress diligently and adjust goals as needed to stay on track.

5. Develop a comprehensive strategy outlining roles, responsibilities, and accountability for achieving results. Provide employees with the necessary tools, resources, and incentives to support ongoing alignment and attention to the transformation.

6. Encourage enthusiastic engagement from all employees by ensuring they understand the vision and their role in achieving it. Provide opportunities for employees to work within their strengths and passions, fostering a culture of commitment and dedication.

7. Shift the focus from goals to results, emphasizing accountability and long-term success. Clearly define expected results and identify actions and deliverables required to achieve them. Encourage employees to embrace accountability and align their efforts with the organization's objectives.

8. Combat short-term thinking by fostering a culture that values long-term results and encourages employees to think beyond immediate challenges. Create alignment with clear statements of desired outcomes and redefine accountability within the organization's culture.

By implementing these considerations, leaders can facilitate successful cultural transformation, driving organizational alignment, engagement, and sustainable results.

# 5

# Accountability must be re-defined

The Cambridge Dictionary defines accountability as *"Someone who is accountable is completely responsible for what they do and must be able to give a satisfactory reason for it."* Would you agree that this definition reads judgemental instead of aspirational? This definition may also induce fear in employees for their ability to achieve or provide a "satisfactory reason" for not achieving their goals. People often see failure as unfavourable, and most people will reduce their risk of being negatively judged at work. Can you blame them? If you define accountability as above, there is nothing good about not achieving our desired results, which, in my experience, is incorrect; there is so much to learn.

I have read many definitions of accountability in my research on this topic. The one that stands out for me, defined by the authors of The OZ Principle, is *"a personal choice to rise above one's circumstances and demonstrate the ownership necessary for achieving the desired results."* To achieve a state of personal and collective accountability. Employees who understand that it is a personal choice to rise above it all consistently ask themselves, "What else can I do to move positively past the current conditions to achieve the desired results"? The impact: an exceptionally successful organizational culture where employees take action proactively, "ballooning" your organization to a place only in your dreams[19]

I have had the pleasure once in my career to work with a leadership team, small as we were, that was completely aligned. The magic created when we brainstormed solutions to organizational problems was an experience I hadn't had before or since. I would suggest we were the "dream team," with employees lining up to figure out how to join our team. So how did we do it? In many ways, but first, we were jointly accountable for supporting employees in achieving the outcomes within our department instead of our silos.

## Why Joint Accountability is Critical

When I discuss my organizational accomplishments, my tagline is "I am not an island, and no one person accomplishes greatness alone." That said, I would testify that no one person is responsible for the successes or failures of organizational results. Results have collective accountability, and organizations function best with Individual Responsibility and Collection Accountability. Additionally, employees have varying strengths, and by combing the strengths and talents of your team members, you allow for learning and development, a reduction of the victim mentality, an increased line of sight to organizational goals, an increase in employee recognition across the organization, and a decrease in silos.[20] Creating teams that understand how to work together to achieve greatness is essential. Train them to work together! Allow teams time to be curious, argue, disagree, storm and norm, and you will discover after they band together to achieve their outcomes that they are remarkable.

Leaders must carefully approach team composition, leveraging each member's unique strengths to foster collaboration and drive exceptional outcomes. By understanding their teams' talents and capabilities, leaders can strategically integrate diverse skills, unlocking the potential for extraordinary results. This deliberate approach enhances productivity and cultivates a sense of joint accountability among team members.

In addition to optimizing team dynamics, organizations can foster a culture of accountability through employee mentorship programs and cross-departmental collaboration initiatives. These initiatives provide opportunities for employees to engage with colleagues from different areas of the organization, gaining insights into varied perspectives and approaches. Such interactions solidify the notion of collective accountability, encouraging individuals to prioritize the organization's overarching goals over individual departmental interests.

In one of my past organizations where I worked, I witnessed the transformative power of cross-departmental collaboration. To enhance leadership development across the organization, a team comprising members from different departments was assembled to design comprehensive training programs. Through collaborative brainstorming sessions and shared expertise, this cross-functional team developed tailored training modules that resonated with leaders across various business units. The result was a dynamic learning environment, with over 120 leaders actively participating in skill-building exercises and knowledge-sharing sessions. This collaborative endeavour strengthened leadership capabilities and fostered a culture of collective accountability, where individuals felt empowered to contribute to the organization's overall success.

By strategically aligning team composition and promoting cross-organizational collaboration, leaders can instill a sense of accountability that transcends departmental boundaries, driving organizational excellence and fostering a culture of shared success.

## Reflection Questions

1. How can leaders integrate diverse team talents effectively to achieve extraordinary results?

2. What strategies can be implemented to foster collaboration across departments and promote a culture of joint accountability?

3. Have you experienced successful cross-organizational collaboration in your work environment? If so, what were the key factors that contributed to its success?

4. How can mentorship programs enhance employee collaboration and understanding of joint accountability concepts?

5. What steps can leaders take to ensure all employees feel accountable to the entire organization rather than just their division?

# 6

# Accountability Generates Cultural Transformation

Many leaders understand that the most effective organizational culture is where accountability is more about empowerment than punishment and that allowing autonomy for results creates motivated employees.[21] But how do you do that? Is there an easy way forward?

There is no easy way forward, but accountability will improve organizational results beyond imagination when re-defined and applied effectively. Employees will continually rise above the Victim Cycle, eagerly "star in the solution," and focus on what they can do to keep moving things forward.

Employees thrive on innovation, constantly seeking fresh and creative solutions by asking themselves, "What more can I do to contribute to the solution?" In this environment, ideas abound, and problems are seen as nothing more than opportunities in disguise—just waiting for a ray of sunshine to illuminate the path forward. And you, dear leader, are that ray of sunshine!

However, fostering a culture of empowerment and accountability requires more than just redefining the concept—it demands a deeper understanding of human behaviour and interpersonal dynamics. This is where emotional intelligence comes into play. Emotional intelligence, or EQ, encompasses the ability to recognize, understand, and manage our own emotions and those of others. Leaders with high emotional intelligence are better equipped to navigate the complexities of organizational culture and foster an environment where accountability thrives.

By developing emotional intelligence skills, leaders can inspire and motivate their teams, cultivate a sense of ownership and responsibility, and facilitate open communication and collaboration. Furthermore, emotional intelligence enables leaders to navigate challenges with empathy and resilience, fostering trust and cohesion within the organization.

In the upcoming sections, we'll delve deeper into the role of emotional intelligence in shaping organizational culture and driving accountability. Through practical insights and strategies, we'll explore how leaders can cultivate their emotional intelligence to create a culture where accountability is not just a buzzword but a fundamental aspect of organizational success.

## Has your Brain Ever been Hijacked: The Need to be Emotionally Intelligent?

Have you ever had a colleague or friend who displays quite a bit of emotion and continually gets worked up about things you feel are not a big deal? Sure, of course, who hasn't? Well, without knowing them and making a big assumption, it may be that these folks just are not very aware of what is happening in their brains when things get stressful; they are not "Emotionally Intelligent."

That said, to ensure accountability in your organization, Emotional Intelligence or Emotional Quotient (EQ) is one of the most critical workplace behaviours. It boosts both employees and leaders' performance, communication, and motivation. As defined by J. Freedman,

> *"Emotional Intelligence is a way of recognizing, understanding, and choosing how we think, feel, and act. It shapes our interactions with others and our understanding of ourselves. It defines how and what we learn; it allows us to set priorities; it determines the majority of our daily actions. Research suggests it is responsible for as much as 80% of the "success" in our lives."*[22]

Appropriately, EQ requires up-front attention when considering cultural transformation, as it will be nearly impossible for someone to focus on results and accountability if their EQ is low. Studying EQ will support employees in all aspects of the Cultural Transformation and is the "single biggest predictor of performance in the workplace and the strongest driver of leadership and personal excellence."[23] Those highly skilled at EQ are better able to give and receive feedback and engage in effective and innovative brainstorming amongst colleagues, improving performance across the organization. How experienced are you at EQ? Some days, I am very skilled; other days, maybe not as much. There are many factors to consider, such as sleep, nutrition, and stress levels at home and work, and leaders must be thoughtful when employees seem a little out of sorts.

When embarking on a cultural transformation journey, EQ deserves upfront attention. After all, it's challenging to prioritize accountability when individuals struggle to manage their emotions effectively. By investing in EQ training, organizations equip their employees with the tools to recognize and regulate their emotional responses, paving the way for enhanced performance and collaboration.

Imagine Sophie, a dedicated project manager, undergoing EQ training with her team. As they develop self-awareness and self-management skills, they learn to navigate conflicts constructively and communicate more effectively. This newfound EQ strengthens their relationships and fosters a greater sense of accountability towards shared goals.

But EQ isn't just about personal growth—it's also about promoting critical thinking within the organization. By encouraging employees to "check their brains in at the door," leaders foster a culture where individuals feel empowered to think critically and challenge assumptions. Through workshops and discussions on critical thinking themes, employees learn to approach problems with curiosity and creativity, unlocking innovative solutions and driving organizational success.

Consider implementing the Eight Elements of Critical Thinking, developed by Stephen R. Covey, within your organization. By fostering a culture of intellectual curiosity and open-mindedness, you empower employees to question the status quo and explore new possibilities. Employees strengthen their critical thinking skills through ongoing training and reinforcement, driving continuous improvement and innovation.

Nonetheless, you can help your employees become more skilled at recognizing when their brains are hijacked by implementing training in EQ, as this skill is flexible and developable. When you are proficient at EQ, the pathway that information travels in the brain remains free of barriers, and you strengthen the "connection between the rational and emotional centers of the brain. The more you think about what you are feeling – and do something productive with that feeling - the more developed the pathway becomes."[24] There are four critical EQ skills all employees should possess, organized into personal and social skills, including:[25]

## Personal ability

- *Self Awareness* – the ability to accurately perceive your emotions at the moment and understand how you commonly react to challenges, specific events, people
- *Self Management* – the capability to use self-awareness to manage your emotional reactions to circumstances and individuals

## Social ability

- *Social Awareness* – the ability to accurately detect emotions in others and understand what is going on with them
- *Relationship Management* is the product of the above combined emotional intelligence skills and is your capacity to understand your and others' emotions to interact successfully.

## Check-In Your Brain at the Door

Emotional Intelligence and critical thinking are foundational skills for building a culture of accountability and results. By investing in EQ training and promoting critical thinking within the organization, leaders empower their teams to navigate challenges with confidence and creativity, driving long-term success and growth.

In addition to employees and leaders with high EQ, it is essential to encourage employees to stop "checking their brains at the door" and use their intelligence to think critically through their problems. Leaders can promote critical thinking within their teams; however, training employees to improve this critical competency is also essential. Offering attention upfront in the process will only support you in changing your culture to one focused on accountability and results through improved thinking in the workplace. Just imagine the possibilities!

Stephen R. Covey developed the Eight Elements that frame thinking, providing an excellent framework for employee development[26]. The framework serves as a valuable tool for supporting employee development. These elements offer a structured approach to enhancing thinking skills within an organization, promoting intellectual curiosity and open-mindedness. By focusing on themes such as self-awareness, integrity, empathy, and critical questioning, the framework encourages employees to challenge assumptions, think creatively, and explore new possibilities. Ultimately, Covey's Eight Elements offers a comprehensive framework for fostering a culture of critical thinking and continuous improvement within the workplace.

All leaders should consider the implications of a command-and-control organizational structure on employee engagement and critical thinking. In such environments, where employees are told what to do without room for questioning or exploration, valuable insights and innovative ideas generated by employees often go unexplored.

Take Sophie from the beginning of our story, a proactive team member who consistently raises thought-provoking questions during team meetings but feels stifled by the rigid hierarchy. Despite her enthusiasm and creativity, Sophie's ideas are seldom acknowledged or integrated into the project workflow. As a result, valuable opportunities for innovation and problem-solving are missed, and the organization needs to tap into the full potential of its workforce. This highlights the importance of fostering a culture that encourages critical thinking and empowers employees to contribute their ideas and insights, ultimately driving innovation and organizational success.

According to experts in critical thinking, it only takes 30 days to change your mind, and by considering one idea or theme a week, leaders can start to guide the way within their team meetings and one-on-one interactions with staff. In addition, employees can be encouraged to explore each topic more deeply as it relates to them and further strengthen their critical thinking competency[27]:

As we conclude this chapter, let's transition from reflection to action by outlining several ideas for implementing change in our organizations. These strategies are aimed at fostering a culture of empowerment, accountability, and innovation:

1. Invest in comprehensive training programs emphasizing empowerment, emotional intelligence, and critical thinking. Equip leaders with the skills and tools necessary to create an environment where accountability thrives.

2. Conduct workshops and seminars focused on enhancing emotional intelligence among employees at all levels. Provide practical exercises and resources to help individuals effectively recognize and regulate their emotions.

3. Introduce initiatives that promote critical thinking skills across the organization. Encourage employees to question assumptions, challenge the status quo, and explore new perspectives through workshops, discussion forums, and brainstorming sessions.

4. Develop clear and transparent accountability frameworks that outline expectations, responsibilities, and consequences. Ensure accountability is integrated into performance management systems and reinforced through regular feedback and recognition.

5. To promote innovation and problem-solving, Foster collaboration and knowledge sharing across departments and teams. Encourage

interdisciplinary projects and initiatives that leverage diverse perspectives and expertise.

6.  Cultivate a continuous learning and development culture where employees are encouraged to seek out new skills and knowledge. Provide access to training resources, mentorship programs, and learning opportunities tailored to individual needs.

7.  Establish open and transparent communication channels that facilitate feedback and dialogue between leaders and employees. Encourage constructive feedback, active listening, and two-way communication to foster trust and accountability.

8.  Implement recognition and rewards systems that acknowledge and celebrate accountability, innovation, and performance excellence. Recognize individuals and teams who demonstrate exceptional leadership, problem-solving skills, and initiative.

By implementing these ideas, we can create a workplace culture where empowerment, accountability, and innovation are not just ideals but integral aspects of organizational identity and success.

# You Must Care Passionately About Your People

**7**

Before discussing how to gain accountability across your organization, it is valuable to note a few things. First, employees want employers and leaders who care about them as humans and are as committed to them as they are to you. They want leaders who believe in them, are honest to a fault, are focused on helping them succeed, and are there for them when they need it, personally and professionally - "and rightfully so."[28] As a leader of leaders, I continually stress the importance of considering the human factor in leadership. I want my leaders to care as much about their people as I care about them, and it is vital for all leaders to fully understand the psychological impact they have on their staff's lives—both excellent and terrible. As quoted in the Oz Principle,

> *"A leader should possess human understanding and consideration for others. Men/women are not robots and should not be treated as such. I do not mean by any means to suggest coddling. But men/women are intelligent, complicated beings who respond favorably to human understanding and consideration. By these means, their leader will get maximum effort from them. They will also get loyalty."*[29]

Showing you care also means providing honest and helpful feedback. You do your employees no favours by covering up their limitations. Of course, providing direct and valuable feedback in a not personal way is not always easy, and many leaders need help giving feedback as much as employees wrestle with receiving it. One of my most terrifying moments as a leader was in one of my past roles after being promoted to supervise my previous colleagues; I had to provide feedback to a team member who had performance issues impacting the rest of the team. I was a young leader, and this employee was what I would call a bully. I was terrified, but I understood I would be doing this employee no kindness by not helping her see how her words and actions impacted her and her co-workers' results.

Accordingly, early in my leadership career, I recognized that being exceptionally skilled at giving and receiving feedback is crucial to be accountable. I have found that having some ground rules helps to set the stage with staff, and the following Four Agreements can help to create a positive experience for all:[30]

1. *Use your words delicately*; to yourself and others when giving and receiving feedback.

2. *Do not take anything personally*; watch for signs of ego and fear.

3. *Do not make assumptions*; be curious, ask clarifying questions to ensure you understand the feedback received and supply valuable feedback in return.

4. *Always do your best!* Remember your best changes daily, and be kind to yourself and others.

## Scenario: Fostering Accountability Through Human-Centered Leadership

Tabatha, a seasoned leader at the Cool Coffee Club, was recently promoted to a managerial role overseeing a team of dynamic individuals. With her new responsibilities, Tabatha recognized the importance of fostering a culture where accountability was not just a buzzword but a lived experience for everyone in her team.

Reflecting on her journey as a leader, Tabatha understood that gaining accountability across the organization required more than just policies and procedures—it required genuine care and empathy for her team members.

She believed that employees wanted leaders who cared about them as individuals and were committed to their personal and professional success.

One day, during a team meeting, Tabatha noticed that one of her team members, Mark, seemed disengaged and uninterested in the discussion. Sensing that something might be bothering him and Tabatha took a moment to pull him aside after the meeting.

In a private conversation, she approached Mark with empathy and compassion, expressing her concern for his well-being. She encouraged him to share any challenges he might face and assured him she was there to support him.

As Mark opened up about some personal struggles he was experiencing outside of work, Tabatha listened attentively, offering encouragement and understanding. She reminded Mark that the team was there to support each other through professional and personal challenges.

Later that week, Tabatha followed up with Mark to check on his progress and see if there was anything else she could do to support him. She also provided constructive feedback on ways he could improve his work performance, emphasizing the importance of accountability and teamwork.

Through Tabatha's genuine care and support, Mark felt valued and motivated to overcome his challenges and contribute positively to the team. Tabatha's leadership style, rooted in empathy and accountability, created a culture where team members felt empowered to take ownership of their actions and outcomes, driving success for the organization as a whole.

# 8

# Lasting Accountability – It is Attainable

How do we create a culture where rules are unnecessary, and all employees are accountable for their results? I am sure you have tried a method or two, as have I. However, after significant research and analysis, I propose a technique adapted and modified from my work on results-based accountability and *"The Steps to Accountability"* found in the *Oz Principle*[31]. *As* shown in Graphic Five and described below, I have created a framework for attainable and lasting accountability that includes five easy-to-implement steps to guide your employees and leaders to excellent results. I challenge you to take your organization on the journey; you won't be disappointed.

# THE 5 PATHWAYS TO ACCOUNTABILITY

YOUR JOURNEY TO SUCCESS

**STAY DEDICATED**

**TAKE CHARGE**

**STAR IN THE SOLUTION**

**MAKE IT HAPPEN**

**STAY ON TOP**

# Pathway 1. Stay Dedicated

When employees Stay Dedicated, they concentrate on staying positive when challenges arise and focus on their accountability and how they use their words. Dedicated employees remain focused on priorities and seek and are open to the feedback and opinions of others, allowing them to see reality bravely.[32]

During the Stay Dedicated step, employees must feel safe to have the courage to be completely honest with themselves by recognizing when they fall into the victim cycle, limiting their ability to see reality. It is hard sometimes to face reality, and staying in a bubble may feel safe and is undoubtedly less risky; however, it does not allow employees to move to the *Take Charge* phase to achieve results. Is this due to fear of failure and judgment? Perhaps, no one likes to fail, but employees need to understand how being honest with themselves and seeking feedback increases their tendency to focus on the results.

Employees must feel comfortable enough to seek as many viewpoints as more viewpoints equal, reducing biases and having the ability to see reality from many different sides. Employees should be encouraged to use their EQ skills, avoid taking anything personally during their discovery, and instead focus on being empowered by what they learn. Listening carefully and asking clarifying questions is essential to prevent assumptions that support learning.

Lastly, employees should be encouraged not to nullify feedback but to thank the brave for using their voices. Leaders must also recognize when employees "get hijacked" to avoid miscommunication. When provided feedback, I am the type of person who can sometimes get offended first if I have not had time to think about it and consider any truth. Any leader who doesn't allow me time to absorb and digest feedback may not successfully convey the message. You also may have employees like me, those A+ students who strive for perfection and do not like not getting it right!

# Pathway 2. Take Charge

How often have you had a problem and many great ideas to solve it, but something stops you or your team from getting it done? Once employees run down the first pathway and are confident they understand reality fully, you must encourage them to move to the next step and Take Charge. When employees Take Charge of their circumstances, they accept full ownership of past and present behaviour, moving them away from the Victim Cycle and improving their future situation.[33] Selective accountability will not allow employees to move into this step. Leaders must support all employees in being accountable for good and bad results, recognizing there are always excellent lessons in our misses. As discussed above, this will require employees to feel safe enough to seek feedback from many stakeholders during the evaluation and be curious to learn more by asking clarifying questions.

## Cultivating a Culture of Openness and Collaboration

Further to seeing and owning opportunities in areas of influence, all employees should be encouraged to speak up when ideas are present about any part of the organization. Every employee can support organizational goals and solutions to problems, and new innovative ideas and advancement can come from anywhere; be open to listening to everyone.

Have you ever had a great idea to solve a problem outside your sphere of influence, only to be aggressively shut down with a "how dare you get in my business"? If you have experienced this, I am sure you were as disheartened as I was, and to rise above it all, we need to take a cue from the author Alexandre Dumas, "All for one and one for all, united we stand, divided we fall!"[34] The sooner organizational leaders realize that it is not a competition but a collaboration of all the best brains in the room, the better off everyone will be.

## Overcoming Barriers to Action

What will get in the way of employees taking action? There are many barriers to success, including the crucial role of psychological safety, that I will discuss next. Still, if you help employees connect current circumstances with what has been done or not done and tie future events with what they will do, you will have helped employees assume full accountability. I am sure you have likely heard before, "If you're not part of the solution, you are part of the problem."[35] As indicated, all employees need to be open to hearing feedback in a non-threatening way. Once this shift takes place, and accountability is no longer a bad and scary, employees can cruise down the pathway to stardom.

# The Crucial Role of Psychological Safety in Cultivating Accountability

How do employees undergo such a transformative shift? This question resonates deeply with both myself and Dr. Amy Edmondson, a distinguished professor at Harvard Business School and author of 'The Fearless Organization.' Dr. Edmondson's research and writing on psychological safety within organizations have profoundly illuminated its critical role in nurturing effective teamwork, driving innovation, and promoting organizational learning. Through her work, our understanding of how psychological safety contributes to organizational performance and success has been significantly enriched.

As Dr. Edmondson illuminates, psychological safety serves as the bedrock upon which a culture of accountability is built. It encompasses the shared belief within a team or organization that members feel secure in taking interpersonal risks, expressing their ideas, and voicing their concerns without fear of reprisal or judgment. This environment empowers employees to speak up, share innovative ideas, and take ownership of their actions, facilitating accountability and driving organizational progress.

## Fostering Trust and Open Communication

Employees feel empowered to express themselves openly and honestly in an organization where psychological safety thrives. They are confident that their colleagues and leaders will welcome and value their ideas, concerns, and feedback. This trust and open communication environment creates a foundation for accountability, as individuals feel secure in owning their work and outcomes. Employees are more inclined to collaborate, innovate, and take calculated risks, knowing they have the support and respect of their peers and superiors. As a result, teams become more cohesive and productive, driving organizational success and achieving sustainable results.

## Encouraging Risk-Taking and Innovation

Psychological safety encourages risk-taking and innovation by creating a space where employees feel empowered to experiment, make mistakes, and learn from failures without fear of repercussions. In such an environment, individuals are likelier to take initiative, challenge the status quo, and propose creative solutions to problems, driving continuous improvement and growth.

## Empowering Ownership and Responsibility

Moreover, psychological safety empowers employees to take ownership and responsibility for their actions and outcomes. When individuals feel safe to speak up and take calculated risks, they are more likely to hold themselves and others accountable for achieving shared goals and delivering results. This sense of ownership fosters a culture of accountability, where individuals take pride in their work and are committed to achieving excellence.

## Building Resilience and Adaptability

Furthermore, psychological safety builds resilience and adaptability within teams and organizations. By creating an environment where individuals feel safe to express their concerns and learn from failures, teams can bounce back quickly from setbacks, adapt to changing circumstances, and thrive in dynamic and challenging environments. This resilience is essential for maintaining accountability during times of uncertainty or adversity.

## Fostering Psychological Safety: An Organizational Example

Imagine a team meeting where a new project proposal is being discussed. In a psychologically safe environment, team members feel comfortable sharing their thoughts and ideas openly, without fear of judgment or reprisal. One team member suggests a creative approach to solving a particular challenge, even though it deviates from the usual process. Instead of being met with skepticism or criticism, their idea is met with curiosity and interest from their colleagues.

As the discussion continues, other team members build upon the initial idea, offering their insights and perspectives. Even with disagreements or differing opinions, everyone feels heard and respected. The team leader facilitates the conversation, encouraging participation from all members and emphasizing the importance of diverse viewpoints.

By the end of the meeting, the team has developed a comprehensive plan that incorporates elements of each member's input. There is a shared sense of ownership and commitment to the project, as everyone feels valued and included in the decision-making process.

This example illustrates how psychological safety enables teams to collaborate effectively, innovate, and achieve better results. When employees feel safe speaking up and sharing their ideas, it fosters a culture of trust, respect, and accountability within the organization.

In conclusion, psychological safety is a fundamental prerequisite for creating a culture of accountability within any organization. By fostering trust, open communication, and empowerment, psychological safety enables individuals to take ownership of their actions, embrace risk-taking and innovation, and build resilience in the face of challenges. Leaders must prioritize creating and maintaining a psychologically safe environment to support accountability and drive organizational success.

# Pathway 3. Star in the Solution

Once psychological safety is established within the organization, teams and leaders can confidently embark on the "Star in the Solution" pathway. This pathway prioritizes tackling genuine organizational challenges, rather than implementing change for the sake of it. It's crucial to emphasize that this step isn't about creating busywork or disrupting processes unnecessarily. Instead, the focus remains on maintaining a problem-solving mindset aligned with organizational goals. Encouraging employees to explore additional solutions empowers them to take ownership of their actions and attitudes. Furthermore, fostering open communication ensures a comprehensive understanding of the problem by incorporating diverse perspectives. Leaders and employees should collaboratively assess the risks associated with maintaining the status quo versus implementing change, ensuring that any proposed changes align with the organization's vision and objectives.

In addition to the aforementioned elements, it's crucial to incorporate structured decision-making processes, such as the Structured Decision-Making (SDM) approach, to guide research and facilitate informed decisions aligned with organizational objectives. This method offers a flexible framework with step-by-step guidance, ensuring clarity and effectiveness in decision-making processes.[36]

Moreover, embracing change is paramount during this phase. Change inherently evokes fear, resistance, and complaints among individuals. Therefore, prioritizing the "people side" of change is essential. Developing a comprehensive change plan is imperative to successfully navigating through this phase. Failing to prepare adequately may hinder the ability to sway the hearts and minds of employees towards the envisioned transformation"[37]. Change management strategies will be further explored later to provide robust support throughout the transition.

During the evaluation of the current organizational state, it's vital to assess whether employees and leaders exhibit the following behaviours:

• Continually inquire, "What else can I do?"
• Demonstrate complacency by passively accepting the status quo

- Feel empowered to challenge assumptions and beliefs in a safe environment
- Engage in open-mindedness by actively seeking diverse perspectives
- Proactively anticipate potential challenges and risks
- Take initiative and assume accountability in exploring solutions to drive results
- Proactively address any emerging issues preemptively
- Foster a culture of collaboration and brainstorming to tackle organizational challenges.

# Pathway 4. Make It Happen

I love to Make it Happen and get things done, don't you? Pathway 4 allows employees to "have fun by getting it done"! This step has all the action and will enable employees to take full accountability, rise above their circumstances, and achieve desired results. Employees learn to be accountable to accomplish better results, improve individual and organizational outcomes, and, most importantly, avoid the Victim Cycle.[38] Accordingly, Pathway 4 is where employees gain confidence and competence as they navigate new problems and implement solutions. This step is where accountability becomes apparent, not just for activities, circumstances, or feelings, but for the future accomplishment of the company.

I must stress that to fly smoothly down the pathway to Make it Happen, you must consider your level of risk, as a risk-averse organization will rarely make significant strides in accountability. As indicated, no one wants to fail, and if the leaders are not on board to accept risk, staff will be frozen in Step 3. Only by taking risks can you continue to grow as an organization and move from rules to results. Employees need to feel safe to take well-conceived risks through the encouragement and support of their leader[39].

To Make it Happen, everyone must embrace responsibility for results (joint accountability), and employees will:

- Be open and honest and recognize when they are in the Victim Cycle
- Measure and eagerly report on their progress and seek support when stuck
- Clarify expectations and accountabilities, both with leader and co-workers
- Take a "well-conceived" risk without the risk of future obstacles in their career
- Look at challenges as "grumpy opportunities" and work to flip them around
- Continue to look for how they can improve their circumstances
- Use their discretionary time at work to continue to improve
- Keep going until they achieve the desired result

# Pathway 5. Stay on Top

Now that you've achieved the desired results, the challenge becomes maintaining that success. It's essential to recognize that staying on top requires continuous effort, as unexpected challenges can arise at any moment – losing your top employees to a competitor could be akin to a disastrous windstorm.

Pathway 5 represents this ongoing journey, akin to navigating a mountain trail where the path may become unclear, leading to the risk of veering off course. One of the primary challenges lies in effectively capturing, reporting on, and learning from your results, a task that demands determination and may be met with fear of failure from employees. However, having reached this point on the path, it's essential to vigilantly monitor and adjust course as necessary. Step 5 involves developing and implementing a Performance Management Program (PMP) designed to measure organizational performance and facilitate continuous learning. This program is a tool for guiding organizational improvement efforts and is further explored in the subsequent discussion below.

# THE PERFORMANCE MANAGEMENT PROGRAM

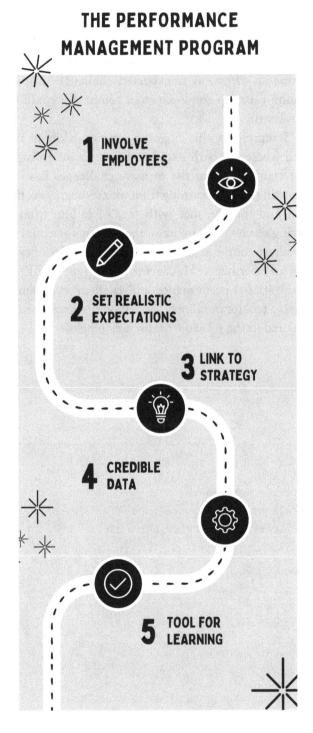

1 INVOLVE EMPLOYEES

2 SET REALISTIC EXPECTATIONS

3 LINK TO STRATEGY

4 CREDIBLE DATA

5 TOOL FOR LEARNING

## Get Employees Involved

I am sure you would agree that all employees need to know what they are accountable for and agree that the goals are achievable. Stretch goals are acceptable and encouraged; however, if employees never achieve them, motivation will decrease faster than they think. Accordingly, it would be best to involve the employees responsible for reporting on results in all aspects of the development of the measures. To create buy-in and credible and honest reporting of results, employees must feel the work is worth the effort and identify what data is crucial to do their jobs effectively. This involvement further encourages ownership, motivation, and commitment to measuring results and a perception that the performance targets are fair and attainable, resulting in better buy-in and use of the data and measures[40]. Have you ever been asked to report upon something where you disagreed that it was essential to your job or output? If yes, did you care about the results? Did they support you in doing your job better?

In addition to supporting effective reporting, involving employees will teach them the importance of data collection in future planning and budgeting. Employees will have the tools to critically examine their results and understand the root cause of success or failure. Can you imagine future capabilities once employees can better address the root cause of good and bad results?

Additionally, creating teams of employees to develop measures for cross-divisional outcomes will create employee networks, a learning and development mindset, and potential succession planning opportunities across the organization. Employees gain the opportunity to learn about other business areas; you never know what interests and ideas are sparked in that discovery. You may find out some folks are in the wrong seats and have passions in other business areas where they can work to their full potential.

## Keep it Real

Have you ever had deliverables at work that were utterly impossible to achieve? I have worked in Municipal Government for most of my career, so I passionately say YES! I believe there is nothing more defeating than unreasonable goals. Consequently, the PMP must outline realistic objectives and expectations for employees and provide appropriate resources to achieve goals. Employees will not buy into the Program unless they feel they can succeed. The data will inform decisions, not necessarily determine them, as there are other variables to consider. Appropriately, as mentioned above, the performance data should enhance employees' ability to see how their work impacts others across the organization, increasing understanding of how programs and services contribute to shared outcomes[41]. Understanding the connection is essential to support joint accountability and reduce silos over time.

Keeping it real by setting sensible goals allows employees to think critically about issues that will support them in moving from focusing on the rules to concentrating on innovation and results. Employees need to understand what they are responsible and accountable for and what level of oversight they have on their projects. Additionally, employees need to know that they are responsible for solutions and must be empowered to discover answers, as discussed in the Critical Thinking section. Specific tactics and actions should be developed and implemented with employees working with the leadership team to ensure goals are not aspirational but SMART (specific, measurable, attainable, realistic, and time-orientated). Appropriately, using baselines, past trends, and available resources, starting with just a few measures, will improve acceptance of the PMP[42]. While completing Cultural Transformation, the last thing you must include is too many Key Performance Indicators that will not improve your ability to manage your business but bog staff down with useless data.

## Connect the Dots

Have you ever given your employees tasks without connecting the dots to the big picture? In addition to setting realistic expectations, the PMP must connect to your organizational strategies and business plans, tailoring the Program based on workgroup needs instead of a one-size-fits-all approach. As with the vision for the organization, the goals and measures selected must show a "line of sight" to operations so all employees can see themselves in the Program, thereby increasing ownership and motivation[43]. You want every employee to see themselves in the plan; even your entry-level staff should understand how much value they add to the corporation and how all roles help achieve results.

Ensuring you have the technical resources to support measuring objectives is also essential. In a previous role, our PMP was understood by only one employee, with the data defined by scribbles on sheets of paper inside a large and unorganized binder. Subsequently, you can see how Information Technology systems (ITS) and a well-defined data dictionary are critical for long-term compliance and reduce decision-making based on poor-quality data[44]. In addition, employees must be involved in planning IT systems and trained on new designs; change management is necessary. Lastly, linking financial and Performance information to measure the Program's cost is vital to ensure the price is worth the data collected. Collecting data is unnecessary if it is not helping you manage your business more effectively.

## Develop the Performance Data Dictionary

Once developed, leaders must link the PMP to their employees' accountabilities, remembering that some outcomes are hard to measure and that data is not the sole source of information on the employees' success. Consequently, PMP accountabilities should consider that some results are beyond an employee's control, and employees should track qualifiable and quantifiable data[45] to appreciate the results of their efforts thoroughly.

Further, developing a practical PMP that supports organizational learning requires that the data produced is credible, trustworthy, and reproducible. Likewise, there is the potential for "organizational cheating," usually observed when employees set undemanding targets, concentrate on some measures at the expense of others, or deliberately manipulate the data in situations where they are held accountable for Performance not within their control. Therefore, sensible measures must be selected and supported by organizational incentives to reduce distorting behaviour. Finally, leaders must devote time to work with employees to ensure the information is credible.[46]

## Concentrate on Organizational Learning

Performance measurement motivation must come from the desire to learn and improve Performance. Therefore, a practical PMP can engage employees in understanding what it will take to execute future projects and institute a culture of continuous improvement through learning. Accordingly, performance measurement should improve the organization and promote change by developing a supportive learning culture emphasizing evidence-based information. Essentially, it helps the employees understand the why and the root cause, creating enhanced critical thinking skills for future projects.

Although time-consuming, leaders should determine the lesson from the good and the inadequate measures, especially in the case of budget decisions. The focus on learning will develop innovative strategies and a curious and evaluative culture[47]. When your employees are interested, they are better engaged in the business, are more open to feedback, and continually seek to improve through data collection and observation.

In addition to the measures on organizational goals, efforts should include a review of implementing the Cultural Transformation Strategy across all departments. Leaders must be accountable for getting and staying on the bus related to changes in culture, as this will take concerted time and effort.

## Chapter Takeaways: Empowering Accountable for Organizational Success

1. Stay Dedicated:

   • Encourage employees to stay positive amidst challenges and prioritize accountability.

- Foster an environment where employees feel safe to seek feedback and challenge assumptions.
- Emphasize the importance of using emotional intelligence skills and active listening during interactions.

2. Take Charge:

- Support employees in taking ownership of their circumstances and behaviors.
- Promote a culture of inclusive accountability where all employees are encouraged to provide and receive feedback.
- Cultivate openness and collaboration to harness the collective intelligence of the organization.

3. The Crucial Role of Psychological Safety:

- Highlight the significance of psychological safety in fostering effective teamwork and innovation.
- Emphasize the importance of trust and open communication in creating a psychologically safe environment.
- Encourage leaders to prioritize creating and maintaining psychological safety to drive accountability and organizational success.

4. Star in the Solution:

- Empower employees to focus on solving real organizational problems and achieving outcomes.
- Foster a problem-solving mindset by encouraging employees to take initiative and challenge the status quo.
- Overcome barriers to action by promoting openness to feedback and a culture of joint accountability.

5. Make It Happen:

- Inspire employees to take full accountability for their actions and outcomes.
- Encourage risk-taking and innovation by creating a supportive environment where employees feel empowered to experiment and learn from failures.
- Provide resources and support to help employees navigate challenges and achieve desired results.

6. Stay on Top:

- Develop and implement a Performance Management Program (PMP) to measure organizational performance and contribute to learning.
- Involve employees in setting realistic goals and developing measures to ensure buy-in and ownership.
- Connect the PMP to organizational strategies and business plans to enhance alignment and relevance.

7. Develop the Performance Data Dictionary:

- Link the PMP to employee accountabilities and ensure the credibility and trustworthiness of the data produced.
- Concentrate on organizational learning by using performance measurement as a tool for continuous improvement.
- Review and analyze performance data to identify lessons learned and inform future decision-making.

Implementing these accountable steps can help organizations create a culture where rules are unnecessary, and all employees are empowered to take ownership of their actions and contribute to organizational success.

# The People's Side of Change

**9**

As you likely noticed in the Cultural Transformation Framework, Change Management is represented on the arrow that runs across all elements. Change management strategies and tactics must be considered and implemented at each stage and with each person, group, and leadership team. It is just that important, and without an influential "people change" strategy, change may not happen, or it will not last if it does. I am sure you have been part of organizational change in the past. Was it disastrous? If so, can you pinpoint a cause? I would bet a paycheck that the "people side of change" was not managed as effectively as necessary.

# THE CHANGE MANAGEMENT STRATEGY

**PLANNING**

**PROGRAM DEVELOPMENT**

**IMPLEMENTATION**

**MAINTENANCE**

As discussed in the section on vision, everyone in your organization needs to know where you want to go, as your people are your superpower, and without them on the bus, plane, or train, nothing is possible. Likewise, employees are waiting to be aligned, validated, challenged, and desire to understand how they create value. That said, the focus of communicating this new vision and results must be thoughtful and centred on face-to-face communications, and the door must be opened to the leadership team for employees with questions or concerns. Employees will need to consider the new direction, and questions will be plenty and ongoing. Accordingly, providing opportunities at all levels to engage in a meaningful dialogue about what needs to change and how you plan to get there will be essential.[48] Don't underestimate this time; spend extra time with employees.

As emphasized several times, leaders must align their messaging and actions, ensuring everyone sings from the same song sheet. However, despite our extensive efforts outlined in these pages, achieving perfect harmony remains challenging. There have been moments when the chorus almost reached its crescendo, only to be disrupted by discordant voices. But fear not, for you are the conductor of this symphony. With the strategies in this book, you have the baton to orchestrate a harmonious melody throughout your organization, transforming discord into magical harmony.

Remember that change management is a vast and complicated topic, and leaders must consider many factors and take a deep dive into the current state when developing a change plan. The key to constructing a new culture is to induce small changes, which will take slightly longer but will allow people time to learn and decide to engage. Remember that the main challenges in transitioning are often behavioural, with leaders and employees needing to change how they work, which takes time. Sadly, unlike the character "Axe" in Billions, we don't all have a psychologist as a performance coach on staff to guide us in being our best!

With the help of a performance coach or not, "creating a sense of urgency" will engage employees and help them understand the risk of remaining in the current state and the meaningful opportunities of transitioning to the desired future state[49]. Although "creating a sense of urgency" is critical, you can likely attest that resistance to change is often the main reason change efforts fail[50]. I am sure you have seen resistance when you try to change much of anything as employees are invested in the current state. They need time to be convinced and hear how their co-workers feel about the change.

Therefore, it is essential to "form a powerful guiding coalition" by assembling a group of change champions to promote the concept and elicit change across the organization. Graphic 6 outlines the Change Management Strategy Actions and implementation timing suggestions. As with the development of the PMP, employees must be involved in the change transition. Leaders must determine how to maximize their involvement, as employee participation in change is associated with favourable views, reduced resistance, and improved goal achievement.

# Communication is Essential

As we've emphasized, clarity in direction is paramount, as your employees are the driving force behind your organization's success. Without a clear roadmap to the destination, disappointment is inevitable. Employees are eager to align themselves with the organization's objectives, seeking challenges and a deeper understanding of their value proposition. They crave authentic communication from leadership, preferring clarity from the source rather than speculation at the water cooler. Employees want to be active participants in the change process, not passive recipients of decisions imposed upon them.

Strategic precision is key in communicating the new vision and results. The focus is on various channels of interaction, particularly face-to-face communication and fostering an "open door" policy with all levels of leadership. As employees navigate the new direction, questions will abound, requiring thoughtful and consistent messaging across leadership ranks to ensure changes are conveyed positively and effectively.

## The Communications Strategy

To ensure the message is heard and understood, the Cultural Transformation Communications Plan must include several elements, including:

- The use of richly descriptive words that link strategy to desired outcomes
- The use of multiple mediums for communication that is repeated often in different forms

- A description of what is different this time compared to approaches from the past
- A description of "what's in it for the employee."
- A description of what the leadership team is going to do to address employee concerns
- Communications on actions and progress (based on those issues identified by employees)

## Transformation Takes Time

Transformation within an organizational culture doesn't happen overnight. However, when it comes to communicating your new vision and goals to all employees, immediacy is key. Everyone must receive the same message simultaneously to prevent any misinterpretations. Hosting a town hall or all-employee event provides an excellent opportunity to unite everyone with the leadership team, fostering two-way communication and ensuring clarity across the organization. Additionally, such gatherings serve as ideal platforms for planning team-building and trust-building activities, further advancing your organization's journey.

Moreover, consistent opportunities to engage with the leadership team in a non-threatening, unscripted manner are invaluable. These interactions offer a continuous chance to hear employees' perspectives and concerns, formalizing informal discussions and fostering an environment of openness and trust. Understanding the sentiments of your workforce enables leaders to effectively demonstrate the desired behaviors, provide targeted feedback and recognition, and gain insights into departmental challenges that might otherwise go unnoticed.

The following examples demonstrate various strategies organizations can employ to facilitate effective communication during times of change and transformation.

1. Host regular meetings where the leadership team communicates the new vision and goals to all employees. This allows for direct interaction between leadership and staff, fostering transparency and clarity in communication.

2.  Organize team-building and trust-building activities as part of the employee events following the communication of the new vision. These activities help strengthen relationships among team members, enhancing collaboration and teamwork as the organization embarks on its transformation journey.

3.  Implement an open-door policy for all leaders in the organization to provide regular opportunities for employees to engage with leadership in a non-threatening environment. This encourages open communication and allows leaders to listen to employee feedback, address concerns promptly, and gain valuable insights into the organization's pulse.

4.  Be attentive to conversations happening in the organization's "water cooler" or informal settings. These conversations can provide valuable feedback on employee sentiments, allowing leaders to better understand their staff's concerns and perceptions and address them proactively.

5.  Establishing feedback mechanisms, such as suggestion boxes or anonymous surveys, to encourage employees to share their thoughts, ideas, and concerns anonymously. This ensures that even employees who may be hesitant to speak up in person have a platform to express themselves, contributing to a culture of open communication and continuous improvement.

## Stage the Performance: Cultivating Transparency in Leadership Meetings

During my tenure at one organization, I was impressed by the open forum where I could freely sit, listen, and ask any member of the leadership team questions. This setup provided an excellent opportunity to model the behaviours and actions desired by our teams.

Moreover, these open meetings facilitated a deeper understanding of the organization beyond my department, contributing to my comprehension of the business landscape. By removing the veil of secrecy inherent in closed leadership meetings, employees can engage in new experiences, shaping their beliefs and fostering a culture of transparency. Additionally, open meetings mitigate the spread of gossip that often occurs when meeting minutes are not shared[51].

Expanding on the theme of transparency in leadership, here are some additional ideas to foster openness and clarity within the organization:

1. Implement a practice of regular updates and reports from leadership to the entire organization. This could include monthly or quarterly newsletters, email updates, or even video messages from executives sharing key developments, successes, challenges, and plans. Providing consistent updates helps keep employees informed and engaged in the organization's progress.

2. When making significant decisions that impact the organization or its employees, strive for transparency in the decision-making process. This could involve sharing the rationale behind decisions, consulting with relevant stakeholders, and being upfront about potential implications. Transparency builds trust and reduces uncertainty among employees.

3. Make meeting minutes from leadership meetings and decision-making sessions accessible to all employees. This practice promotes transparency by allowing staff to understand the topics discussed, decisions made, and actions planned by leadership. It also encourages accountability and ensures that information is not confined to a select group.

4. Provide leaders and managers with training and resources on the importance of transparency in leadership. This could include workshops on effective communication, conflict resolution, and building trust within teams. Equipping leaders with the skills to foster transparency can positively impact organizational culture.

By implementing these strategies, organizations can create a culture of transparency where information flows freely, trust is strengthened, and employees feel valued and informed.

## Engage and Inspire: Crafting Memorable Narratives

Crafting memorable narratives is crucial, especially as you navigate through transforming organizational culture. Many employees struggle to articulate how they align with strategic organizational goals, leading to muddy understanding, particularly in entry-level positions.

In their book "Made to Stick," Dan and Chip Heath offer a method to create compelling stories that stick in people's minds. This method, though requiring some initial investment in training, yields remarkable results[52]. I've witnessed its impact when introducing it to a diverse group of 285 employees, from plumbers to the leadership team. The outcome was nothing short of transformative, with each employee crafting their personalized elevator pitch on how they contribute value to the organization and its constituents. The newfound motivation and inspiration among staff were palpable.

While training on the "Made to Stick" principles is ideally conducted at an all-staff event, you can start applying the method to your communications on the transformation journey. It's essential to recognize that changing the message requires a concerted effort, especially considering employees' "curse of knowledge," where they find it challenging to imagine not knowing what they already know. However, by providing experiences like all-team workshops, we can shape new beliefs and gradually mitigate the curse of knowledge over time[53].

The Success method outlines six **fundamental** principles for developing **memorable narratives:**

1. Simplicity: Keep ideas clear and to the point. Focus on the main message without adding extra details. Prioritize what's important, like the saying "a bird in the hand."

2. Unexpectedness: Surprise people with your ideas. Go against what's expected to catch their attention.

3. Concreteness: Make ideas easy to understand and remember. Use sensory details and actions to clarify your message.

4. Credibility: Make your ideas believable. Use trustworthy sources and vivid examples to build trust.

5. Emotional: Connect with people's feelings. Talk about things that matter to them and relate to their emotions.

6. Stories: Use stories to inspire and motivate. Share examples that resonate with people and encourage action.

Below the SUCCESs method support creating a sticky story for the results-based framework we have been discussing in this book.

1. **Simplicity:**

    - Core Idea: The results-based framework empowers employees to take ownership of their work and drive meaningful outcomes.
    - Lead: In our organization, we're simplifying accountability and driving results with a clear and focused framework.
2. **Unexpectedness:**

    - Surprise Element: Imagine a workplace where every team member is fully engaged, accountable, and aligned towards achieving shared goals.
    - Challenge Expectations: "Forget about bureaucratic processes and finger-pointing; our framework transforms how we work together to deliver results.
3. **Concreteness:**

    - Sensory Details: With the results-based framework, each employee knows their role, responsibilities, and the specific outcomes they're accountable for.

- Reduce Ambiguity: No more vague objectives or unclear expectations; our framework provides clarity and direction for every task and project.

4. **Credibility:**

- Authority: Developed and refined by industry experts and tested in real-world environments, our framework has a proven track record of success.
- Vivid Details: Teams that adopt our framework have consistently exceeded targets, improved efficiency, and fostered a culture of accountability and excellence.

5. **Emotional:**

- Appeal to Emotions: Experience the pride and satisfaction of seeing your hard work translate into tangible results that drive the success of our organization.
- Matters to People: At our company, we understand the frustration of working in environments where accountability is lacking. That's why we're committed to providing a framework that empowers every employee to make a meaningful impact.

6. **Stories:**

- Rich Examples: Meet John, a project manager who struggled to keep his team focused and motivated. With our results-based framework, John's team rallied around clear objectives, surpassed milestones, and delivered their project ahead of schedule.
- Inspiration and Connection: From entry-level employees to senior executives, our framework creates a shared language and mindset that unites us in pursuit of excellence. Together, we're rewriting the story of what's possible for our organization.

This sticky story vividly illustrates the transformative power of the results-based framework. It's not just about streamlining processes or setting targets; it's about fostering a culture of accountability, collaboration, and excellence that permeates every aspect of our organization.

As you implement this framework, remember that simplicity is vital. Strip away unnecessary complexities and focus on what truly matters: driving results and empowering your team members to thrive. Embrace the unexpected and challenge the status quo. Don't be afraid to shake things up and push the boundaries of what's possible. These moments of surprise and innovation will propel your organization forward.

Ensure concreteness in your communications. Use tangible examples, clear language, and relatable anecdotes to bring your key messages to life. Make it easy for everyone to understand their role, responsibilities, and the collective vision we're striving to achieve.

Build credibility through transparency, consistency, and authenticity. Lead by example, and let your actions speak louder than words. When your team sees your unwavering commitment to the framework, they'll trust in its effectiveness and embrace it wholeheartedly. Appeal to emotions and tap into what truly motivates your team members. Show them how their contributions make a difference and inspire them to take ownership of their work. Celebrate successes, acknowledge challenges, and foster a sense of belonging and purpose.

Finally, craft compelling narratives that capture the essence of your culture. Share stories of resilience, innovation, and collaboration that resonate with your team members and reinforce the values that define us. By weaving these stories into your communications, you'll create a narrative that inspires, motivates, and unites us in our pursuit of excellence.

# 11

# The Devastating Impact of Bad Leadership

To truly transform your organization's culture, the senior leadership team must be aligned and ready to adapt their approach to meet employees' needs better. Research and best practices consistently emphasize that leadership is the cornerstone for cultural change. In this section, we address leaders at all levels, emphasizing those who lead other leaders. Senior leaders must serve as coaches and mentors, nurturing our teams and empowering them to achieve their utmost potential.

Emphasizing the critical role of effective leadership cannot be overstated; it stands as the linchpin in the transformation of an organization from adherence to rules to the achievement of tangible results. Over my extensive 25+ year career, I've unfortunately borne witness to this phenomenon more times than I can enumerate, and each instance remains unacceptable from my perspective. While I've had great mentors in my career, it's disheartening to see uninspiring leaders among family, colleagues, and friends. Their impact is clear—negative effects like reduced self-confidence drained energy and decreased motivation.

For leaders entrusted with guiding other leaders, a new era of thinking must dawn, reshaping entrenched beliefs and transforming actions. It's crucial to grasp that every decision made in the workplace ripples through our team members' lives, leaving lasting positive and negative impacts. The toll exacted by ineffective leadership on talented individuals undeniably dampens spirits and motivation. Hence, the call for a revolution in leadership practices grows louder—where merit, not tenure, guides promotions and where employees find solace in workplaces brimming with trust and empowerment.

In essence, the pivotal role of effective leadership in driving organizational transformation cannot be overstated. Throughout my journey, I've witnessed firsthand the dire consequences of lacklustre leadership, igniting a genuine call for change. As leaders, especially those steering other leaders, we shoulder the mantle of fostering a culture steeped in coaching and mentorship. It's imperative to realize that the bedrock of cultural transformation lies in the unity and adaptability of the senior leadership team.

Embarking on this transformative odyssey demands a willingness to embrace fresh perspectives and acknowledge our actions' profound impact on our teams, both within and beyond office walls. The forthcoming chapter delves into transformational leadership, charting a course for leaders to emerge as change catalysts, igniting the flames of inspiration within their teams.

## Transformational Leadership

Through my research on leadership, I found that only some specific strategies I studied were perfect; however, elements of transformational leadership combined with a focus on trust, motivation, and empowerment appear ideal for transitioning the organizational culture. Graphic 7 illustrates the Results-Based Transformational Leadership Model. The model defines results-based transformational leaders as individuals who can create a clear and compelling vision, develop trust and goal clarity, encourage a developmental and innovative culture, reward innovation and achievement, tolerate failure and mistakes, coach and mentor, and encourage purposeful performance information.

**TRANSFORMATIONAL LEADERS**

STEP 1: CREATE A COMPELLING VISION

STEP 2: WORK TO BUILD TRUST

STEP 3: ENSURE GOAL CLARITY

STEP 4: ENCOURAGE INNOVATION

STEP 5: REWARD ACHIEVEMENTS

STEP 6: ACCEPT WELL-CONCEIVED MISTAKES

STEP 7: ACT AS A COACH AND MENTOR

Cultural Transformation requires all leaders to be engaged in the planning and program development, as leaders will be responsible for implementing the tactics within their sphere of influence. Transformational Leaders (TLs) support the speed of change through their ability to foster organizational and cultural change and enhance employee satisfaction, motivation, and performance by delivering the vision while modelling transparent decision-making[54]. Further, TLs exhibit optimism and consistency between their words and actions, encouraging employees to remove their self-interest and focus on their goals[55]. Are you embodying the qualities of a Transformational Leader? If your team were to evaluate how consistently and effectively you demonstrate these skills, what rating would you receive? Ideally, you'd aim for a perfect 10 out of 10. If there's room for improvement, don't worry—there's more to discover in the following discussion.

To initiate the cultural transformation journey, comprehensive training on every aspect of the *Cultural Transformation Framework* becomes imperative for propelling the organization forward. As highlighted earlier, leaders must possess or cultivate competencies in critical areas. To seamlessly integrate this learning, consider crafting a series of targeted workshops strategically delivered within leadership team meetings and other existing time slots. The aim is to maximize the utilization of available sessions, ensuring that the additional training doesn't burden leaders with extra responsibilities. Recognizing the demands on leaders' schedules, it's crucial to assess priorities and grant them the flexibility to offload specific responsibilities, avoiding any undue strain on their already hectic days.

Further, improving leadership competency in applying all the methods we discuss must occur in real time, simultaneously with implementing the rest of the tactics, and must be targeted at what your current leaders need most first.[56] Accordingly, a first assessment of leaders' skills against the recommended competencies below should prioritize learning and development actions.

## Essential Competencies for Leadership Excellence

- Critical thinking
- Change management
- Effective communication
- Emotional intelligence

- Developing employees

- Employee engagement

- Coaching and mentoring
- Effective delegation
- Effective listening
- Critical conversations / focused feedback
- Open and transparent communication
- Diversity & Unconscious Bias at Work

# Empowering Change and Leadership Mastery

Change requires time, preparation and actionable steps. Prepare for transformation by providing:

1.  Continuous Feedback Mechanisms: Establish regular channels for ongoing feedback, encouraging open communication and adaptability.

2.  Inclusive Leadership Practices: Emphasize the importance of diversity, equity, and inclusion in leadership, fostering a culture that values different perspectives.

3.  Employee Well-being Initiatives: Incorporate programs or policies that support employees' overall well-being and promote a healthy work-life balance.

4.  Collaborative Problem-Solving: Encourage teamwork and collaborative problem-solving sessions to harness the collective intelligence of the organization.

5.  Skill-Building Workshops: Provide opportunities for continuous learning and development, focusing on both technical and soft skills relevant to the organizational goals.

6.  Strategic Learning Pathways: Allocate dedicated time for training, focusing on honing skills in effective communication, vision sharing, and competency development.

7.  Leadership Excellence Expectations: Establish clear expectations for leaders, fostering competency growth through structured career dialogues and developmental pathways.

8.  Elevated Accountability: Cultivate heightened accountability with regular performance discussions that ensure consistently delivered planned actions, reinforcing the notion that coaching is an ongoing process.

9. Crucial Support and Resources: Provide the necessary support and resources to guarantee success in every facet of the transformative journey.

10. Holistic Coaching and Mentoring Programs: Implement comprehensive coaching and mentoring training, delving into the nuanced details of these crucial leadership skills (further details discussed below).

11. Innovation Recognition Platforms: Foster a culture of innovation by creating opportunities for rewards and recognition, celebrating the achievements that drive positive change.

12. Appreciation and Acknowledgment Spaces: Establish regular platforms for employees to acknowledge and appreciate each other, contributing to a positive and collaborative work environment.

# 12

# Fostering Trust: The Keystone of Transformative Leadership

Establishing and nurturing trust is pivotal in the intricate dance between leaders and employees within private and public organizations. It's a delicate equilibrium, arduous to forge yet remarkably fragile. Trust, the bedrock of effective relationships, hinges on confidence in an individual's integrity and capabilities. Its absence fosters unease, hampers success, and heightens the risk of misinterpreting intentions and actions.

Throughout my leadership journey, I've underscored to fellow leaders the paramount importance of cultivating trust within their teams. This involves developing trust in leaders and creating opportunities for team members to build trust among themselves. How is this achieved? The journey commences by recognizing each employee as a unique individual. Behind every role lies a person with goals, visions, ideas, passions, and, often, delightful quirks that contribute to a vibrant team dynamic.

Additionally, trust is one of the most potent forms of motivation and inspiration because you can give people greater autonomy for results. Don't worry; they will seek support and guidance if they get stuck.[57] I believe your employees will thrive on trust, and according to a passage in "Contented Cows Still, Give Better Milk,"

*"Trust in those around us acts as a powerful lubricant. It accelerates our work, thoughts, and processes, and its absence puts a measurable drag on all we do. People simply can't execute with speed and precision when operating under an excel of dubious assumptions. The contrast between working in an environment of trust and its opposite is analogous of that of driving on a reasonably straight highway on a clear, dry day versus doing so on a serpentine mountain road on a foggy night."*

I have worked in high and low-trust organizations, and you can see and feel the difference. In a place of **low trust** with employees, it is typical for reduced speed in work output and increased costs for the organization. Employees will not use their "discretionary time at work" to achieve more significant results. Alternatively, in a **high-trust** relationship, there is increased speed in work output and reduced costs overall. Employees show passion for their jobs and continually think about their work, even at home, maximizing their ability to excel in their careers continuously. Further, as the Trust tax and Trust dividend theory indicate, "a company can have an excellent strategy and strong ability to execute, but the net result can be either torpedoed by a low-trust tax or multiplied by a high-trust dividend."[58] The difference is in the employees!

You can be sure to create a trust tax if you take your employees for granted, don't communicate changes effectively, humiliate them in front of anyone, or if you lie to them.[59] Further, in a low-trust organization, you can expect[60],

- A toxic culture with plenty of dysfunction, lawsuits, grievances, sabotage
- Painful micromanagement and bureaucracy
- Redundant hierarchy and powerful political atmosphere
- Many dissatisfied employees and stakeholders
- Significant employee turnover
- Guarded employee communication and dispersing of information
- Silo's
- Hidden agendas
- Excessive time waste and excuses

In a high-trust organization, however, you can expect:

- Positive energy and positive people
- A focus on work
- Effective collaboration and execution
- Positive partnerships
- Innovation and creativity
- Healthy Workplace
- Positive, transparent relationships with employees and stakeholders
- Fully aligned systems and structures
- Learning focus with mistakes seen as opportunities for learning
- A focus on looking for and leveraging each other's strengths

In comparing the two workplaces, the distinction between a low-trust and a high-trust environment becomes starkly evident. In the former, where trust is a rare commodity, employees are often burdened by a high trust tax. This tax manifests in various forms, from increased bureaucracy and micromanagement to a lack of autonomy and stifled creativity. The atmosphere is suspicious, leading to a diminished sense of ownership and commitment. Conversely, a high-trust workplace is a haven for collaboration, innovation, and personal growth. Here, employees are empowered with trust and given the autonomy to excel in their roles. Leadership, systems, and structures are designed not as constraints but as enablers, fostering an environment where individuals thrive. The choice becomes clear — the workplace that trusts its employees to bring their best selves forward, supported by effective leadership and conducive systems, stands out as the more desirable and rewarding professional landscape.

In the pursuit of fostering a culture of trust within teams, numerous authors emphasize the pivotal role leaders play in establishing and maintaining credibility. This necessitates a commitment to authenticity and consistent logic, as advocated by Steven M. R. Covey's Four Cores of Credibility— Integrity, Intent, Capabilities, and Results as shown below[61]. As we delve into the intricacies of trust-building, it becomes evident that these principles form the bedrock of effective leadership, creating a foundation upon which teams can thrive[62].

## Four Cores of Credibility[63]:

1. **Integrity:** Leaders must embody unwavering honesty and a commitment to ethical conduct, fostering a culture of trust within their teams.

2. **Intent:** Demonstrating pure intentions and a genuine concern for the well-being of others establishes a foundation of trust and credibility.

3. **Capabilities:** Leaders should showcase the competence and skills required for their roles, instilling confidence in their teams regarding their ability to navigate challenges.

4. **Results:** Building trust is reinforced by delivering tangible results, showcasing a track record of success that aligns with the team's goals and expectations.

In addition to the Four Core's as described above, there are "13 behaviours that are common to high-trust leaders" that have been grouped into themes that contribute to building and maintaining trust within a team, including:[64]

**Foundations of Trust Building:** These behaviors focus on establishing a positive and open communication environment, fostering continual improvement and trust.

- Effective Feedback
- Demonstrate Respect
- Create Transparency

**Accountability and Integrity:** This group emphasizes the importance of acknowledging mistakes, being accountable for actions, and consistently delivering on commitments, contributing to a culture of responsibility and reliability.

- Right Wrongs

- Practice Accountability
- Keep Commitments

**Leadership Traits Reinforcing Trust:** These behaviors showcase leadership qualities such as loyalty, resilience, clarity, active listening, and trust extension, which collectively build a foundation of trust and contribute to a positive team dynamic.

- Show Loyalty
- Deliver Results
- Confront Reality
- Clarify Expectations
- Listen First
- Learn from Mistakes
- Extend Trust

## The Trust Traingle

Aligned with the work that Covey completed on Trust, the Trust Triangle[65]. The Trust Triangle outlines three core drivers for building and maintaining trust: authenticity, logic, and empathy. Trust is established when individuals believe they are interacting with the real, authentic person, have confidence in their judgment and competence, and feel genuine care for their well-being. When trust is compromised, it often relates to a breakdown in one of these three drivers. The concept of the Trust Triangle underscores the significance of balancing authenticity, logic, and empathy to create a trustworthy leadership dynamic.

## Strategies for Deepening Your Understanding

Beyond the fundamental Four Cores and the delineated 13 behaviors, a toolbox of resources is available to enhance your understanding of your team members. A particularly effective approach involves organizing bi-weekly face-to-face meetings with your team. This dedicated time not only facilitates discussions about work-related matters but also provides a window into their lives beyond the office. Recognizing any commitments or challenges they might be facing at home fosters a more comprehensive connection with your team, contingent on their comfort in sharing such information.

Notably, my friend Gerry Madigan has authored an insightful book titled "TMI – The Ten Minute Interview," emphasizing the significance of acquainting yourself with your staff. I highly recommend giving it a read. Furthermore, it's perfectly acceptable to let your employees know you on a personal level. Humanizing your leadership by acknowledging mistakes and emphasizing your role as a supportive figure in their quest for excellence contributes to a more authentic and mutually beneficial working relationship.

Completing an assessment, such as Strengths Finders 2.0[66] will help all parties gain a deeper understanding of their natural talents and strengths. This assessment, coupled with the proposed team workshops and individual coaching sessions, presents an excellent opportunity for candid conversations and a more thorough exploration of how each employee contributes to the organization's objectives through their distinct strengths and talents. For instance, in a recent workplace, a colleague shared that their leaders initiated a team-wide StrengthsFinder assessment and provided coaching sessions for all staff. This proactive approach demonstrates the organization's commitment to understanding the individual and collective strengths of their team members to provide optimal support.

In addition to Strengths Finders, various tools and assessments facilitate meaningful conversations between leaders and employees regarding their strengths and preferred working styles. Instruments such as Myers Briggs, DiSC, Insights, EQi, and EQi360 offer a comprehensive understanding through a 360-degree review, fostering collaborative strategies to achieve organizational goals while enhancing trust in both leaders and employees. Beyond assessments, another impactful approach involves hiring a coach to collaborate with teams for a predetermined duration. Drawing from personal experience, in one of my past roles, our leadership team engaged with a coach, both collectively and individually. This experience was immensely rewarding, significantly contributing to our team-building efforts.

It is critical to open avenues for richer conversations and deeper insights into individual and collective strengths within a team. These approaches not only enhance collaboration but also contribute to achieving organizational goals and fostering a culture of trust.

## The Art of Giving Feedback

Leaders need to be incredibly skilled at providing the proper feedback at the right time to ensure their message, as intended, is heard and understood by the employee. On the flip side, leaders must also be very skilled at listening to employees and asking questions to seek further understanding. During face-to-face sessions, leaders must create experiences that change employees' beliefs about themselves and their contribution to the corporation's goals.

Additionally, leaders must tell their employees the truth to support their growth. Leaders must be comfortable with being uncomfortable when they must deliver bad news as this ensures they make staff growth a priority.[67] Likewise, feedback must include a plan for concrete ways to move forward and improve and how you will support them. Have you ever encountered employees who were previously told by their leaders that they are perfect? If yes, then you should help them to improve their strengths and weaknesses by providing honest feedback in areas they need to work on. Several steps can guide leaders in ensuring they are focused on creating positive experiences while providing focused feedback to employees that induce change, including:[68]

1. Identify the idea/belief you need to change in the employee

    a. Test the hypothesis, ask for observations, restate what you heard
    b. Ask – What do you think? Why do you believe that? What would you do?
    c. Gain alignment on results and actions

2. Tell them the idea/belief you want them to hold or the behaviour you want them to change

    a. Put it in the context of the vision / goals / results / accountabilities

3. Describe how you will help

    a. Convince people you mean what you say and that you will follow through
    b. Be specific on your proposed actions

4. Ask them for feedback on if what you propose is enough

    a. Allows you to learn what you can do better or if there is more you can do

5. Seek regular feedback during face-to-face meetings on your approach, style, and follow-through.

    a. Employees need to know you want to hear what they have to say
    b. Do not take anything personally, but look for opportunities for growth

## A Strengths-Based Coaching Approach

Leaders have a significant role in supporting employees in developing critical thinking skills, and using a Strengths-Based Coaching Approach instead of solving employees' problems supports this goal. Your employees know the answers to their problems; they just need to be encouraged, and as indicated by John Buchan, "The task of leadership is not to put greatness into people, but to elicit it, for the greatness is there already."[69] Therefore, a coach engages and empowers people to develop the confidence to creatively solve issues on their own utilizing their experience, the experience of others, or other means[70].

Why focus on strengths? Strengths-based coaching supports positive employee engagement while assisting employees in understanding their "superpowers" and how the organization and its stakeholders value those.

It further allows employees to gain increased belief in their abilities, improving confidence and providing significant motivation to excel.

Nonetheless, I understand the desire to quickly and easily get employees out of your office by solving their problems as they arise. Regardless, this keeps employees stuck in a "tell me what to do" cycle where they will not develop innovative solutions that they remain accountable to deliver. As soon as you tell someone what to do, they do not own it, and they cannot create that conscious connection for accountability in their brain. If you have children of pretty much any age, I am sure you can easily understand that concept!

Coaching supports creating new neural pathways, which lead to lasting and sustainable change. Further, a coach approach tends to put people in a state where their brains are more open to learning, visioning, and growth[71]. Coaching also supports employees in developing a growth mindset gaining improved strengths proficiency, frequency of use, and regulation of use (not letting a strength become a weakness).[72]

Additionally, it is helpful to adopt a consistent coaching approach within your entire organization that all leaders can apply to ensure reliability amongst your leadership team. The last thing you need is a few skilled leaders and others who lack the skills necessary to create empowered, innovative, critical thinkers. Leaders who coach their employees are noticeably different from leaders who solve employees' problems for them, and as you can imagine, this type of leadership unreliability produces frustration amongst employees. Can you think of an occasion in your career where this has occurred? I can, and I can attest that the results are less than desirable, and employees spend much time "fence looking" in envy of their colleagues. A method such as that described in Graphic 9 can support your leaders in excelling in this crucial competence[73].

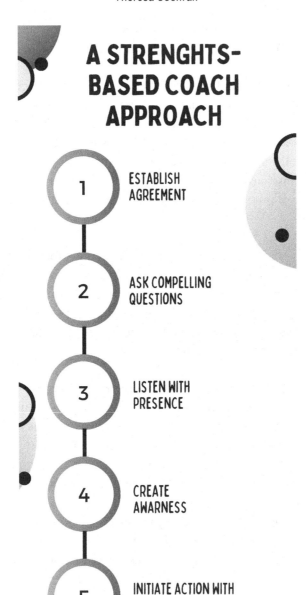

# A STRENGHTS-BASED COACH APPROACH

1 ESTABLISH AGREEMENT

2 ASK COMPELLING QUESTIONS

3 LISTEN WITH PRESENCE

4 CREATE AWARNESS

5 INITIATE ACTION WITH RESPONSIBILITY

# 13

# Training is for Everyone

In the next section of the Cultural Transformation Framework, our attention shifts to all employees. As leaders, we need to have high expectations for our employees with a training and development plan to help them achieve all they are capable of; "then – and only then – can we get ourselves out of their way…and let them get to work!"[74] Additionally, employees want to know that their leader cares about their future growth and, as suggested, will increase their discretionary time working on organization goals. They pleasantly can't stop thinking about work and are significant contributors to results.

Employees need to be more involved in the business, and it will be essential to train them in potentially different ways than in the past. Firstly, it will be necessary to:

- Identify future desired state and determine current employee strengths and skills
- Identify missing job competencies by reviewing job profiles and discussions with employees
- Identify gaps in current staff complement and identify employees looking for growth and development
- Identify what workshops and individual training events are currently taking place and determine alignment

Several other training opportunities will begin to crack away at the current culture by creating new ideas and conversations in the workplace, including:

- Diversity and Unconscious Bias at Work
- Emotional Intelligence

- Psychological Safety
- Insights / DiSC / Myers Briggs
- Performance Management (data not people)
- Active Listening / Communication
- Critical Conversations
- Facilitation skills
- Change management

## Are your Employees in the Right Seat

Further to developing your employees, it is necessary to look at your current staff complement and determine if they are working in the proper role. Are your staff inspired, motivated, challenged, or instead destructively negative, bored, uninspired, past their prime, and looking for a new position? If the latter is true, it is essential not to let a "superstar" slip through your fingers by understanding your team and what they have to offer. Potentially there is another role in the organization that will be a better fit, one where the employee can work to their strengths and passions. I have taken specific jobs to gain further competency and learning, not necessarily because the role inspired me. Should my strengths not have been identified for other more challenging positions, I most certainly would not have stayed in that particular organization for nearly 20 years.

## What about Recruitment

All the tactics and strategies we have discussed will support you in keeping the superstars you have; however, all leaders know that attracting and retaining employees who demonstrate superior competencies is becoming more and more difficult. It is often tricky to find a suitable candidate, and it is not unusual to post important roles more than once to attract the best candidate. Accordingly, most leaders will argue that success in today's business environment requires prioritizing recruitment, as it is essential to hire the best employee right up front. Hiring the best up-front is often tricky as resumes are not a great indicator of the person behind the paper, and excellent candidates can slip through the cracks. That said, a solid look at recruitment practices will be necessary to ensure you see the potential in your candidates.

As we conclude this chapter on fostering change and leadership excellence, it's essential to translate our insights into actionable recommendations. Building upon the principles discussed, these recommendations offer practical guidance for leaders to implement within their organizations. By embracing these suggestions, leaders can accelerate the cultural transformation journey and empower their teams to thrive in an environment of continuous growth and development.

1. Begin by clearly defining the future state of your organization and assess the current strengths and skills of your employees.

2. Review job profiles and engage in discussions with employees to identify any gaps in required competencies.

3. Identify employees who are seeking growth and development opportunities within the organization.

4. Evaluate existing workshops and individual training events to ensure they align with organizational goals and employee development needs.

5. Introduce various training programs to initiate new ideas and conversations in the workplace. Some suggested topics include Diversity and Unconscious Bias at Work, Emotional Intelligence, Psychological Safety, Performance Management (data-focused), Active Listening/Communication, Critical Conversations, Facilitation Skills, and Change Management.

6. Assess whether employees are in the right roles based on their inspiration, motivation, and ability to contribute positively to the organization. Consider reassigning roles to better match employees' strengths and passions.

7. Recognize the importance of hiring the best candidates upfront to ensure organizational success. Review recruitment practices to

enhance the selection process and identify potential candidates who may not stand out on paper but possess valuable qualities for the role.

By taking these actions, leaders can cultivate a culture of continuous learning, growth, and alignment

# 14

# Don't Forget to Build your Brand

Would you say that your organization has a reputation as a great place to work, where employees are motivated each day to achieve their very best? Don't be upset if you say no to that question. Many organizations are not great places to work, and even a few that I would call an "employer of last resort – places where nobody with any brains, ability, or motivation would want to work!"[75]

Sadly, these organizations are typically staffed with "the best of the worst" employees, and it is a challenge to start turning the culture curve. Nonetheless, occasionally they attract some unknowing super-stars, who get dragged down into the depths of frustration for some time until they eventually realize they made a mistake and move on. I have been there. It was not fun.

More scary is that the employees that stay may be the ones continuing to drag down your brand, being content to continue to coast along, only doing the bare minimum to keep their jobs. I can honestly attest that these employees are a real challenge to change!

That said, as we discussed in the recruitment section, it is critical to spend substantial time upfront to ensure you hire employees who will fit into your culture or, in some cases, help advance your culture. Likewise, it is necessary to focus on hiring employees who seem naturally happy and positive, have the potential to be productive and satisfied in the environment, and stay content through growth in your organization.[76] Over time, this will support rebuilding your brand as a great place to work.

## Shareholder Trust Strengthens Your Brand

Have you ever taken a job where your friends looked at you like you were crazy due to the business's reputation? When I took a job in an organization with a terrible reputation as an employer, a colleague asked, "Why was I going to the dark side." Naively, I thought I could have a lasting impact!' but as I have indicated, it takes more than one dedicated person to change a well-ingrained culture.

Accordingly, for your employees to achieve results and attract only the best employees, citizens, stakeholders, and customers, trust is essential. When you are trusted as an organization, you see an increase in innovation, collaboration, partnering, execution, and loyalty. In the absence of this reputation, it is a challenge to move any project forward, as past practices will undoubtedly provide a cloud over the organization's ability to be successful in the future. In one organization I worked, some residents would come to open meetings and loudly criticize the organization and its leaders and staff. I am sure you can imagine how this made the team feel about their contribution to the residents and their chosen current purpose.

Shareholder trust requires you to examine your reputation honestly and focus on the organization's external brand. Improving your brand has many benefits, but the best one is that employees will be proud to work for the organization and demonstrate enhanced ownership and accountability for their work[77].

# 15

# Remarkable, Motivated, Empowered & Inspired Employees!

To reiterate, wouldn't it be great to have all your employees happy to be at work, motivated to do their best, always learning, and growing, all the while supporting and collaborating with their diverse and intelligent colleagues to solve problem after problem? Of course, your answer is definitely! If employees are happy and productive, leaders can free up their time on the underperforming employees and instead work to support those "hitting home run after home run".

To kickstart transformation within your organization, it's crucial to ensure that everyone understands the underlying reasons driving the change. This involves presenting a compelling case for change and conducting an assessment of the current organizational culture. Additionally, leaders should actively engage in targeted discussions, promote diversity and inclusion, establish a Cultural Transformation committee, organize relevant events, and foster a culture of appreciation and recognition. These initiatives lay the groundwork for meaningful and sustainable change within the organization.

## The Case for Change

It is essential to create a case for change that ideally speaks to most of the employees in the organization to encourage enhanced ownership for supporting the Transformation. Employees need to hear from leaders face to face and want to understand why change and why now. Best practices for creating this case include[78]:

1. Explain the why and why now

2. Help employees understand what's in it for them (WIIFT)

3. Give the change a timeline, expectations, checkpoints

4. Keep the message simple and repeatable, but ensure you include facts and figures as applicable

5. Tell employees what will change if you are successful. How will you know you're done

6. Be open to dialogue – keep it positive and non-confrontational, and set ground rules

7. Get people involved

## Current Culture Check

A Cultural check-in provides a "pulse check" for how employees feel at a single point within the year and provides a baseline measure of the current state to measure against in the future. Consequently, it is essential to develop a survey to capture baseline data on several issues, including but not limited to how employees feel/think about their:

- value to the organization
- involvement in decisions making
- autonomy for results
- opportunities for growth and development
- diversity in employees and leaders
- appreciation for contributions
- leaders' ability to lead

Capturing a baseline allows for developing specific actions and tactics to address the low-score themes and build upon the topics employees feel are working. Some steps could include:

- Complete a strength and weaknesses analysis (SWOT or TOWS) with various employees from all levels to understand the current state and develop strategies and actions to address the lower levels of engagement
- Build upon previous activities that were successful into the new Cultural Transformation strategies and tactics
- Develop areas of high satisfaction through targeted actions
- Create communications on the meaning of the Cultural Transformation survey questions to ensure there is a common understanding of the meaning
- Check in regularly with employees to discuss actions and progress
- Monitor the success of implementation and address any challenges and issues

## Building Momentum: The Power of Focused Conversations

While feedback has been extensively discussed in the leadership section, we've yet to tap into the collective wisdom dispersed throughout the organization. All employees must engage in focused conversations, fostering growth and learning without egos or hurt feelings. When I mention "focused conversation," I envision employees sharing insights in a manner that fosters mutual understanding of each other's skills and strengths, ultimately driving organizational learning. These discussions shouldn't be confrontational or hurtful but rather inquisitive, supportive, and productive.

Facilitating "focused conversations" is multifaceted. While I've only begun to scratch the surface of this strategy, bolstering employees' ability to engage in such dialogues is paramount to advancing the culture. Employees must feel empowered to speak openly and honestly, having had ample time to prepare and focus their discussions by understanding the topic and the questions they wish to explore. Moreover, it's essential to encourage employees to prepare for these conversations by extending invitations and seeking consensus for their occurrence. The overarching goal should always be learning, with positive outcomes, to strengthen relationships and enhance organizational performance.

To cultivate a culture of effective communication within your organization, it's essential to provide opportunities for skill development and relationship-building. Workshops are instrumental in achieving this goal, offering tailored sessions to enhance employees' communication prowess and strengthen team connections. By leveraging these workshops, organizations can empower their workforce to communicate more effectively, fostering collaboration, productivity, and overall success. Below are some actionable strategies to advance communication skills and cultivate a cohesive team environment:

1. **Communication Workshops:** Host workshops focused on enhancing communication skills such as active listening, effective feedback, and conflict resolution. Provide practical exercises and scenarios for employees to practice these skills in a safe environment.

2. **Team-Building Activities:** Organize team-building activities that encourage collaboration, communication, and problem-solving. These could include outdoor retreats, team challenges, or virtual team-building exercises tailored to remote teams.

3. **Developing a Common Language:** Implement a glossary of common terms and phrases used within the organization to ensure clarity and consistency in communication. Encourage employees to use this language in meetings, emails, and day-to-day interactions.

4. **Cross-Departmental Collaboration:** Facilitate cross-departmental collaboration sessions where employees from different teams can come together to discuss projects, share ideas, and learn from each other's perspectives. This promotes understanding and strengthens communication across the organization.

5. **Communication Tools and Platforms**: Provide employees with access to communication tools and platforms that facilitate

seamless communication, such as project management software, instant messaging apps, and video conferencing tools. Offer training sessions to ensure employees are proficient in using these tools effectively.

6. **Peer Coaching and Mentorship Programs:** Establish peer coaching or mentorship programs where employees can receive guidance and feedback from their peers or more experienced colleagues. This fosters a culture of continuous learning and development while improving communication skills.

7. **Regular Feedback Sessions:** Schedule regular feedback sessions between managers and employees to discuss communication strengths and areas for improvement. Encourage open and honest dialogue, and provide actionable feedback to help employees enhance their communication skills over time.

8. **Role-Playing Exercises:** Conduct role-playing exercises during team meetings or training sessions to simulate real-life communication scenarios. This allows employees to practice their communication skills in a low-pressure environment and receive constructive feedback from their peers.

By implementing these strategies, organizations can empower their employees to communicate more effectively, strengthen team connections, and foster a culture of collaboration and mutual respect.

# 16

# Embracing Diversity: Overcoming Unconscious Bias in the Workplace

Addressing diversity and unconscious bias in the workplace isn't just a task; it's an opportunity for transformative growth and unparalleled success. While it's undeniable that navigating this terrain can pose challenges, the rewards of embracing diversity are boundless. Imagine a workplace where every individual's unique perspectives, backgrounds, and experiences come together to drive innovation and excellence. That's the vision we aspire to realize.

By championing diversity and inclusivity, we pave the way for richer collaboration, deeper empathy, and more creative problem-solving. It's about harnessing the power of diversity to propel our organization to new heights, where every voice is valued, and every individual thrives. Yes, change can be daunting, and staying in the comfort of the status quo may seem easier. However, the journey toward a more diverse and inclusive workplace is one worth embarking on—a journey that promises not only to transform our culture but also to elevate our results to unprecedented levels of success.

Accordingly, maintaining the status quo regarding diversity and unconscious bias at work is detrimental to your organization's future and hinders your managers' ability to be as creative as possible with their teams and results.[79] Yes, diversity and unconscious bias are sensitive and complex to discuss at work. No one wants to say or do the wrong thing. Further, unconscious bias is not just about race but also about gender, age, financial status, ability, religion, education, culture, geography, sexual orientation, and socioeconomic background[80], which requires you to be very thoughtful in tackling the issue. Consequently, the information herein will only touch the surface on the subject in hopes that you take the time to learn as much as you can about increasing diversity and reducing unconscious bias in your organization.

Stacey A. Gordon, the author of *Unbiased, Addressing Unconscious Bias at Work*[81], is an expert in the area, and I would recommend her book to everyone. Gordon defines unconscious bias "as a way for us to quickly categorize other people without thinking and as a shortcut our brains take, which is affected by social, cultural, and religious norms." It is crucial to consider and identify what norms impact your organization's results before moving forward.

For nearly two decades, I had the privilege of working within a large and diverse organization where embracing diversity was not just a value, but a fundamental aspect of our culture. There, efforts to reduce bias and promote diversity permeated every level, from the frontline staff to the executive boardroom. In that environment, fostering inclusivity seemed like second nature, and I assumed this was the norm across all organizations.

However, my perspective shifted when I transitioned to a smaller company. As I sat in discussions with the executive leadership team about the importance of diversity among our employees, I was taken aback by a comment made by one of my colleagues. They expressed a sentiment of being "tolerant" of other cultures and claimed not to have felt biased in their candidate selection process. But upon reflection, I couldn't help but question the implications of using the term "tolerant." Does it suggest that diversity is something to be endured rather than celebrated? And does it inadvertently reveal a subtle bias in our approach to hiring and inclusivity?

This realization prompted me to delve deeper into the complexities of diversity and unconscious bias in the workplace. It became evident that while some organizations may believe they are inclusive, there is often room for improvement and a need for more nuanced understanding. Thus began my journey to advocate for meaningful change and foster a workplace culture where diversity is not just tolerated but embraced and celebrated for the invaluable contributions it brings.

Accordingly, it is crucial to understand the organization's current state related to its diversity from top to bottom. Further, it is essential to understand what "unconscious bias" exists in your culture and your employees thinking and behaviours and provide training and opportunities for advancing this topic as often as possible. Gordon delivers a Blueprint for organizations to utilize while working on this critical change in her book. The Blueprint includes four steps:[82]

1.  **Create Awareness**—Dig deep to determine your current state through surveys, focus groups, one-on-one meetings, and town hall meetings. Assess the current state of diversity and trust in the organization.

2.  **Align to your Strategy** – once you have the data you need, formulate a plan to incorporate the tactics to tackle what you learned in step 1 into your overall Cultural Transformation strategy.

3.  **Take Action**—Review and revise all policies, guidelines, practices, and procedures to determine any bias. According to Stacey, "Action is determining why 30% of your workforce is diverse, yet a white man fills every leadership role."[83]

4.  **Create Advocacy**: Align everyone to the strategy, educate all staff, and check in regularly to determine areas of concern.

In conclusion, fostering diversity and addressing unconscious bias within your organization is not just a matter of good practice—it's a necessity for driving innovation, creativity, and success. To embark on this journey of change, organizations must first assess their current state of diversity and identify any unconscious biases that may be present. This involves creating awareness through surveys, focus groups, and one-on-one meetings to understand the organization's culture and employees' perceptions.

Once armed with this knowledge, leaders can align their diversity efforts with the overall Cultural Transformation strategy, weaving tactics into the fabric of organizational change initiatives. Taking action is crucial—policies, guidelines, and practices must be reviewed and revised to eliminate bias and promote inclusivity at all levels.

However, change doesn't happen overnight. It requires ongoing advocacy and education to ensure alignment with the diversity strategy and address any areas of concern that arise. Gordon's Blueprint offers a solid starting point, but organizations must take significant action and tailor their approach to their unique circumstances.

Ultimately, fostering diversity isn't just about ticking boxes—it's about creating a culture where everyone feels valued, respected, and empowered to contribute their unique perspectives and talents. By embracing diversity and addressing unconscious bias head-on, organizations can pave the way for a brighter, more inclusive future.

In the pursuit of fostering a more inclusive and diverse workplace, it's essential to engage in meaningful reflection and strategic planning. The following questions serve as a guide to assess your organization's current state, identify areas for improvement, and develop actionable strategies to promote diversity and address unconscious bias. By exploring these questions thoughtfully and collaboratively, you can lay the groundwork for positive change and create a workplace culture where all employees feel valued, respected, and empowered to succeed.

1. How would you rate the current state of diversity within your organization, and what evidence supports your assessment?

2. What steps have you taken to identify and address unconscious bias in your workplace?

3. In what ways do your current policies, guidelines, and practices promote diversity and inclusivity? Where do they fall short?

4. How aligned are your diversity efforts with your overall Cultural Transformation strategy? Are there any gaps or areas of disconnect?

5.  What specific actions can you take to revise existing policies and practices to eliminate bias and promote inclusivity?

6.  How do you plan to create advocacy for diversity within your organization, and how will you ensure that all staff are educated and engaged in the process?

7.  What metrics will you use to measure progress and success in fostering diversity and addressing unconscious bias?

8.  How will you handle any resistance or pushback from employees or leaders who may be resistant to change in this area?

9.  What support or resources do you need to effectively implement and sustain diversity initiatives within your organization?

10. How will you celebrate and recognize achievements and milestones along the journey towards a more diverse and inclusive workplace?

As indicated by Satya Nadella, CEO of Microsoft. "Diversity is not just a nicety, it's a necessity. In the tech industry, we need to do better. It's not just the right thing to do; it's also the smart thing to do for our business."

# 17

# Empowering Change Agents: Building a Culture Transformation Team

In addition to the elements already discussed, a Cultural Transformation Team is essential to build a strong and positive culture of engaged and empowered employees and provides an opportunity to concentrate on delivering experiences that reinforce the vision. This type of reinforcement is necessary as change efforts typically fail because those trying to implement the change do not understand the "underground" organizational culture. The informal networks impede the ability to gain traction in any change effort[84].

The "water cooler" has long been a hotbed of rumours and misinformation, fostering fear and anxiety in the workplace. However, there's a silver lining: a dedicated group of employees ready to champion transformation with their unique and creative ideas. After all, employees hold the key to innovation and progress. Every organization has its hidden influencers—those individuals whose support is crucial for driving change. They must play a pivotal role in the Team and subsequent actions, lending their full support to the transformation. Moreover, leaders must actively participate, striking a balance between top-down directives and bottom-up initiatives. As discussed, building trust and fostering collaboration among employees is paramount to success. Great leaders will combine strategic goals from top leadership and tactical involvement by informed and knowledgeable employees at all levels[85]. In essence, the Cultural Transformation Team will take on the following responsibilities:

- Serve as champions for the Cultural Transformation Strategy and its accompanying tactics.
- Organize employee events that accurately reflect the collective voice within the organization.
- Prioritize the creation of experiences that empower employees to spearhead innovative solutions.
- Hold themselves accountable by facilitating lessons learned workshops and celebrating successes.
- Foster collaboration to address cross-divisional challenges and drive innovation.
- Provide support for change management initiatives and actions.
- Aid in the delivery of informal communications to ensure clarity and transparency.
- Play a crucial role in implementing the organization's goals and strategies.

## Building Community: The Impact of Employee Events

Employee events are another critical element of an effective Cultural Transformation strategy. Employee events allow employees to engage in the business and can be used to reward and recognize employees for their contribution to outcomes. Further, events developed and led by employees have a greater chance of success if those involved understand the organization's common goals and the employees' needs. Accordingly, to boost event uptake, the Cultural Transformation Team should develop and lead the events once the leadership team identifies and clearly articulates a vision for the specific event. To enable success, events should have the following:

- A clear and concise vision and expectations from the leadership team
- Participation of the employees involved on the Cultural Transformation Committee and other employees is necessary to achieve the concept of the event
- A focus on engaging employees in the business in exciting and creative ways
- A specific theme that will guide the activities of the event

- Employee-led sessions that reduce the discomfort of employees being "talked at" from a podium
- An opportunity for employees to provide feedback and follow up
- A description of how the organization is changing and what is going to be different
- An opportunity for direct involvement from all levels of employees, allowing members to shape and build the desired culture

## Employee Appreciation is Necessary

Employee engagement is a multifaceted topic deserving of its own comprehensive exploration. It's a complex and deeply personal aspect of organizational dynamics that demands dedicated effort and attention. While this section offers insights and strategies, it's important to acknowledge that effective employee engagement strategies must be tailored to the unique context and individuals within each organization. As highlighted in the introduction, my journey into leadership and Cultural Transformation was ignited by a recognition that there had to be a better way. Year after year, dismal employee satisfaction scores underscored the organization's struggle to achieve optimal results. The prevailing notion that a paycheck sufficed as a reward for a job well done fell short in inspiring and motivating employees to reach their fullest potential. It became evident that true engagement transcends monetary incentives, necessitating a deeper understanding and investment in fostering a culture of genuine appreciation, recognition, and meaningful connection.

Appropriately, employee appreciation, reward, and recognition programs form integral components of an organization's overarching Cultural Transformation strategy. However, it's imperative that organizations rethink their approach to these programs. In this new paradigm, employee engagement practices encompass a broader spectrum of initiatives aimed at ensuring employees are not only content but also highly productive in their roles.

While compensation and rewards certainly play a role, true employee engagement extends far beyond monetary incentives. It encompasses opportunities for involvement, fostering a sense of belonging, involvement in meaningful projects, clear purpose and direction, the ability to demonstrate competence, autonomy in achieving project outcomes, transparent information sharing across the organization, avenues for promotion, involvement in special projects, and robust training and development opportunities[86]. It is essential to recognize that while research has demonstrated that monetary rewards are not always the primary motivator for employees, the absence of financial incentives can significantly impact morale, particularly for those who place value on such rewards. Therefore, within the realm of Cultural Transformation, the role of rewards and recognition is multi-faceted:

- Ensuring employees are empowered to perform at their best by providing them with the necessary support and resources.
- Removing barriers to satisfaction within the organization by fostering an environment where employees feel valued and appreciated.
- Establishing a structured framework for acknowledging and rewarding employees across all levels of the organization for their contributions and achievements.
- Offering opportunities for those motivated by financial incentives to attain them, thereby catering to diverse preferences and motivations among employees.
- Providing avenues for leaders to express appreciation for their team members in varied and meaningful ways, fostering a culture of gratitude and recognition.

Rewards and recognition can be employee motivators; however, as indicated, many things influence employees, and leaders should understand what inspires their staff. Do you know how your employees like to be appreciated for their contribution? Do they like public or private recognition? Would they prefer money or time off? It is essential to know.

Lastly, employees should be recognized for their great ideas and innovative suggestions by formalizing a process to submit ideas on improved techniques or other efficiency and effectiveness ideas to the leadership team for review. Even if ideas are not utilized immediately, they can be captured and documented for implementation later.

# 18

# Empowering Cultural Transformation: The Path Forward

In wrapping up this journey towards Cultural Transformation, it's clear that the road ahead requires dedication and effort. There's no sugarcoating the fact that effecting significant change within your corporate culture demands substantial attention and commitment. The first step lies in grasping the concepts we've delved into and evaluating them against your organization's current cultural landscape.

Taking a cue from Michael Watkins' insightful book, "The First 90 Days," adopting a learning-oriented approach is paramount. Invest time in understanding before taking action, absorbing insights from diverse perspectives within your organization. Embracing a culture of learning will necessitate collective growth through meaningful conversations and widespread comprehension of the changes and their rationale[87].

Guided by the Cultural Transformation Framework, tailored to suit your organization's unique needs, you hold the power to effect positive change and drive results. The envisioned Cultural Transformation Team, in collaboration with leadership, presents a prime opportunity to craft specific actions and strategies to enhance employee engagement.

Anticipate a shift in how employees approach their work each day, reflected in rising engagement survey scores over time. Remember, Cultural Transformation is a journey, not a destination. Implementing new strategies and actions annually, backed by an implementation plan facilitating quick wins and long-term progress, ensures a sustainable shift towards an engaged and empowered workforce focused on organizational success.

In Appendix 1, you'll find recommendations to support your endeavour, offering practical insights to navigate this transformative journey. Lastly, as leaders refocus on maximizing the exceptional talent within their organization, they anticipate a positive ripple effect—fostering a culture where employees thrive, achieving success day after day.

In conclusion, remember the timeless adage, "Either you manage your culture, or it will manage you." By prioritizing your organization's culture, you lay the foundation for lasting results and attract top-tier talent. Embrace this journey as a partnership, and together, you'll ascend to the pinnacle of success.

THE CULTURE REVOLUTION METHODOLOGY

1. DEFINE THE VISION
2. REDEFINE ACCOUNTABILITY
3. COMMUNICATE
4. TRANSFORM LEADERS
5. EMPOWER EMPLOYEES
6. TRAIN EVERYONE
7. EVALUATION & REVIEW
8. CHANGE MANAGEMENT

# Cultural Transformation Dictionary

**Baseline:** Information gathered before implementing a project or programme that establishes an initial position for the organization from which the results achieved in the project or programme are measured (The United Nations Development Group (UNDG), 2010; Friedman, 2005).

**Change Management:** The process of planning, implementing, and managing changes within an organization to effectively transition individuals, teams, and the organization as a whole from the current state to a desired future state. Change management involves communication, stakeholder engagement, training, and support to minimize resistance and maximize the adoption of change initiatives (Prosci).

**Continuous Improvement**: A philosophy and approach focused on continually enhancing processes, products, or services through ongoing incremental changes. Continuous improvement involves regularly reviewing and analyzing performance data, identifying areas for enhancement, and implementing iterative improvements to drive organizational excellence (Lean Six Sigma Institute).

**Diversity, Equity, and Inclusion (DEI):** Diversity, equity, and inclusion (DEI) refers to the practices and policies aimed at creating a workplace environment that embraces and values diversity in all its forms, ensures equity in opportunities and treatment, and fosters a culture of inclusion where all individuals feel respected, supported, and empowered to contribute their unique perspectives and talents. DEI initiatives encompass recruitment and hiring practices that promote diversity, programs to address systemic barriers and promote equity, and efforts to cultivate an inclusive culture where everyone feels a sense of belonging and is able to thrive. By prioritizing DEI, organizations can enhance innovation, employee engagement, and organizational performance while fostering a more equitable and just society (Society for Human Resource Management, 2021; Diversity, Equity, and Inclusion in the Workplace: A Guide for Employers, 2020).

**Emotional Intelligence (EQI):** The ability to recognize, understand, manage, and express one's own emotions, as well as to perceive, interpret, and respond to the emotions of others effectively. Emotional intelligence encompasses skills such as self-awareness, self-regulation, social awareness, and relationship management, and it plays a crucial role in leadership, teamwork, and interpersonal relationships in the workplace (Goleman, D. 1995).

**Empowerment Leadership:** Leadership is about empowering other people as a result of your presence – and making sure that impact continues into your absence (Frei, F & Morris, A. 2020).

**Key Performance Indicators (KPIs):** Specific metrics used to evaluate the performance of an organization, project, or process against strategic objectives or predefined targets. KPIs provide quantitative measures of progress and success, helping organizations track performance, identify areas for improvement, and make data-driven decisions (Balanced Scorecard Institute).

**Organizational Behavior:** The study of how individuals, groups, and structures within an organization interact and behave in the workplace. Organizational behaviour examines factors such as communication, leadership, motivation, decision-making, and group dynamics to understand and improve organizational effectiveness and employee well-being (Robbins, S. P., Judge, T. A., & Vohra, N. 2019).

**Organizational Cheating:** Organizational cheating refers to unethical or fraudulent behaviors carried out by individuals or groups within an organization for personal gain or to achieve organizational goals through deceitful means. This may include actions such as falsifying financial records, misrepresenting performance metrics, manipulating data or information, breaching ethical standards, or engaging in corrupt practices.

Organizational cheating can undermine trust, integrity, and transparency within the organization, leading to adverse consequences such as financial loss, reputational damage, legal liabilities, and erosion of employee morale. Effective measures to prevent and address organizational cheating include promoting a culture of integrity and ethical behaviour, establishing robust internal controls and compliance mechanisms, providing ethics training and education, fostering open communication channels, and enforcing disciplinary actions against perpetrators (Jones, T. M., 1991; Trevino, L. K., & Nelson, K. A., 2011).

**Organizational Culture:** The shared values, beliefs, norms, and behaviours that shape the collective identity and operating principles of an organization. Organizational culture influences how individuals and groups interact, make decisions, and perceive their work environment, ultimately impacting organizational performance and effectiveness (Edgar Schein, Organizational Culture and Leadership).

**Performance Measure:** A measure that provides the data and documentation necessary to determine if a program or service system is working, suggesting whether an organization is achieving its strategy (Friedman, 2005; Sanger, 2013).

**Performance Management:** Performance management encompasses the processes and activities aimed at monitoring, evaluating, and enhancing individual and organizational performance to achieve strategic goals and objectives. It involves setting clear performance expectations, providing regular feedback and coaching, conducting performance evaluations, identifying areas for improvement, and recognizing and rewarding high performance. Performance management systems often include goal setting, performance appraisal, competency assessment, development planning, and performance feedback mechanisms. By effectively managing performance, organizations can align employee efforts with organizational goals, identify and address performance gaps, foster continuous learning and development, and drive overall organizational success (Armstrong, M., & Taylor, S., 2014; Aguinis, H., 2019).

**Performance Monitoring:** A process of securing and analyzing performance data to compare how well a program is doing, focusing on continuous improvement and learning from results (UNDG, 2010).

**Project Management:** The discipline of planning, organizing, executing, and controlling resources to achieve specific project goals within defined constraints such as time, budget, and scope. Project management involves coordinating various activities, tasks, and stakeholders to ensure successful project completion. Key components of project management include project planning, scheduling, risk management, communication, and stakeholder engagement (Project Management Institute, 2017).

**Results-Based Accountability (RBA):** Results-based accountability is a disciplined, action-orientated business philosophy that can be used to improve program and service system performance with a focus on planning, implementation, learning, and reporting (Freidman, 2005; The UNDG, 2010).

**Results-Based Management (RBM):** Results-based management is a managerial discipline that focuses on improving decision-making in the organization through a life-cycle approach that incorporates strategy, employees, resources, and business process with a focus on performance measurement, accountability, learning and adapting, and transparency (Results-Based Management Tools at CIDA, 2013).

**Rules-Based Organization:** Rules-bases organizations are typically hierarchical, command and control organizations in which all aspects of work are well organized and regulated. Accordingly, policies and procedures can in some instances be limiting to enhancing service levels, innovation and continuous business improvement (Mayne, 2010).

**Result or Outcome:** Results are the intended or achieved short-term and medium-term effects of a specific action written in a way that stakeholders can understand. They describe a measurable change in state that occurs based on a cause-and-effect relationship that are intended, unintended, positive and or negative and generate measurable outputs or impacts to citizens (Freidman, 2005; The UNDG, 2010).

**Stakeholder Engagement:** The process of involving individuals, groups, or organizations who may be affected by or have an interest in a project or initiative. Stakeholder engagement aims to gather input, build relationships, and address concerns to ensure that decisions are informed and inclusive (International Association for Public Participation).

**Strategy:** a collection of actions that form the organizational goals and objectives that have the ability to improve results (Freidman, 2005, p. 20).

**Strategic Planning:** The process of defining an organization's mission, vision, goals, and objectives, as well as determining the strategies and actions required to achieve them. Strategic planning involves assessing internal and external factors, setting priorities, allocating resources, and establishing performance measures to guide organizational direction and decision-making (Harvard Business Review).

**Transformational Leadership:** A style of leadership whereby leaders appeal to the importance of collective outcomes by defining a compelling vision that changes employees' beliefs, assumptions or behaviours with the objective of making a positive impact on the organizational culture and inspiring employees to focus on the goals of public service as opposed to their own interest (Moynihan, Pandey, & Wright 2012; Paarlberg, & Lavigna, 2010).

**Unconscious Bias:** Unconscious bias refers to the attitudes and stereotypes that influence our understanding, actions, and decisions in an unconscious manner. These biases can be based on factors such as race, gender, age, ethnicity, or other characteristics, and they can affect our perceptions, judgments, and behaviors without our awareness. Recognizing and addressing unconscious bias is essential for promoting diversity, inclusion, and fairness within organizations. Strategies to mitigate unconscious bias include awareness training, implementing structured decision-making processes, and fostering a culture of openness and diversity (Harvard Business Review, 2016; Diversity and Inclusion Best Practices Guide, 2020).

# Appendix 1

## Strategic Action Plan:
## Transformative Recommendations

**Recommendation 1:** Craft an organization-specific, results-based management strategy and vision, and institute the Cultural Transformation Framework across all facets of the organization.

**Recommendation 2:** Garner support from employees and organizational leaders, including coordinators and team leaders, to ensure widespread commitment to the transformation journey.

**Recommendation 3:** Foster a culture of accountability by implementing the Steps to Accountability alongside a robust Performance Management Program, empowering individuals to take ownership of their actions and results.

**Recommendation 4:** Provide continuous training, targeted feedback, and coaching to supervisors, nurturing transformational leadership qualities essential for steering the organization towards accountability and results-driven practices.

**Recommendation 5:** Conduct a thorough assessment of the existing organizational culture and devise a comprehensive change management strategy, leveraging the involvement of change champions to drive cultural shifts effectively.

**Recommendation 6:** Execute the accountability and results-based principles through a phased approach, offering ongoing employee training to ensure seamless implementation. Utilize a lifecycle planning model to structure Transformation activities, encompassing planning, program development, implementation, and monitoring and evaluation, fostering a culture of continuous improvement and learning.

Numerous actions that must be considered have been developed under each recommendation's sections. Implementation of the recommendations will benefit from a phased approach, utilizing a lifecycle planning model. This approach involves structuring transformation activities into phases, including planning, program development, implementation, and monitoring and evaluation. Additionally, it's crucial to emphasize the importance of communication throughout the process. Clear and transparent communication channels should be established to inform all stakeholders about the transformation efforts, their roles and responsibilities, and progress. Fostering a culture of open feedback and dialogue will further enhance alignment and engagement among employees at all levels. This holistic approach aims to build a continuous improvement and learning culture, ensuring sustained success in cultural transformation efforts.

# In-text Citations

1  Conners, R, Smith T, & Hickman C, *(2010) The Oz Principle, Revised, Revised*, p. 11

2  ", p. 24

3  ", p. 11

4  ", p. 11

5  Web Pro News. Netflix Considers Changes to Its Iconic "Freedom and Responsibility" Culture (webpronews.com)

6  (24) Google's 20% Time: Fostering Innovation and Employee Empowerment | LinkedIn

7  Tjan, A. (2010). HBR. Harvard Business Review. Four Lessons on Culture and Customer Service from Zappos CEO, Tony Hsieh (hbr.org)

8  Patagonia. (n.d.). Case study. Retrieved from https://harbert.auburn.edu/binaries/documents/center-for-ethical-organizational-cultures/cases/patagonia.pdf

9  Cochran, T, (2015), From Rules to Results, A Guide to Cultural Transformation

10  Cochran, T, (2015), ""

11  Conners, R & Smith T (2012), Change the Culture, Change the Game

12  ". p. 155

13  Kotter, J, (2012), Leading Change, p. 71

14  Catlette, B. & Hadden R. (2012). Contented Cows Still Give Better Milk, p. 44

15  ", p. 72 - 74

16  " p. 74

17  Conners, R & Smith T (2012), Change the Culture, Change the Game, p. 33

18  " p. 35

19  Conners, R, Smith T, & Hickman C, *(2010) The Oz Principle, Revised*, p. 47 – 49

20  "p. 52-57

21  Conners, R & Smith T (2012), Change the Culture, Change the Game

22  The Best Emotional Intelligence Quotes of All Time (sourcesofinsight.com)

23  Bradberry, T & Greaves, J (2005). The emotional intelligence quick book, everything you need to know to put your EQ to work, p. 52-55

24  , p. 12

25  ", p. 28 - 31

26  Elder, L & Paul, R (2012). Critical Thinking, A guide for improving every aspect of your life, p. 16

27  " p. 47 - 170

28  Catlette, B. & Hadden R. (2012). Contented Cows Still Give Better Milk, p. 66.

29  As quoted by, Catlette, B. & Hadden R. (2012). Contented Cows Still Give Better Milk, p. 6

30  Ruiz, D, (1997), The Four Agreements

31  Conners, R & Smith T (2012), Change the Culture, Change the Game, p. 22-23

32  Conners, R, Smith T, & Hickman C, (2010) The Oz Principle, Revised, p. 68

33  ", p. 89

34  Alexandre Dumas, as quoted by Bustin, G, Accountability (2014), p.73

35  Conners, R, Smith T, & Hickman C, *(2010) The Oz Principle, Revised*, p. 101

36  Introduction to Structured Decision Making, SDM Fact Sheet (2008) CSP3171

37  Conners, R, Smith T, & Hickman C, *(2010) The Oz Principle, Revised*, p. 115

38  ", p. 135

39  "", p. 135

40  ", p. 27

41  Mayne, 2007; Wimbush, 2011

42  Mayne, 2007

43  Goh, 2012

44  Mayne, 2007, p. 4, p. 138

45  Cochran, T, (2015), From Rules to Results, p. 29

46  ", p. 30

47  ", p. 29

48  Conners, R & Smith T (2012), Change the Culture, Change the Game, p. 169

49  Kotter P, (2012), Leading change

50  Kee & Newcomer, 2008; Erwin & Garmin, 2010

51  Cochran, T, (2015), From Rules to Results, A Guide to Cultural Transformation

52  Heath, C., & Heath, D. (2008). Made to Stick. Arrow Books. p. 10

53  ", p. 16 - 20

54 Ledimo, 2014; Moynihan, Pandey & Wright, 2012; Paarlberg & Lavigna, 2010

55 Kouzes, James, & Posner, 2008; Ledimo, 2014; Paarlberg & Lavigna, (2010)

56 Conners, R & Smith T (2012), Change the Culture, Change the Game, p. 155

57 ", p. 29

58 ", p. 13 & 20

59 Cotlette, B. & Hadden R. (2012). Contented Cows Still Give Better Milk, p. 27.

60 ", p. 23

61 ", p. 41 - 135

62 Frei, Frances X., & Morriss A. (2020) Unleashed: The Unapologetic Leader's Guide to Empowering Everyone Around You.

63 Frei, Frances X., & Morriss A. (2020) Unleashed: The Unapologetic Leader's Guide to Empowering Everyone Around You.

64 ", p. 140 - 229

65 Frei, F. & Morris. A. (2020) Begin with Trust. Havard Business Review. https://hbr.org/2020/05/begin-with-trust.

66 Rath, T. (2007). Strengths finder 2.0. New York: Gallup Press.

67 Catlette, B. & Hadden R. (2012). Contented Cows Still Give Better Milk, p. 85.

68 Conners, R & Smith T (2012), Change the Culture, Change the Game, p. 162

69 John Buchan, as quoted by, Cochran, T. A Strengths-based Coach Approach, Slide 1

70 Cochran, T. A Strengths-based Coach Approach, Slide 7

71 Boniwell, I (2012), Positive psychology in a nutshell: the science of happiness p. 16

72 ". p. 24

73 Cochran, T. A Strengths-based Coach Approach, Leadership Workshop

74 Catlette, B. & Hadden R. (2012). Contented Cows Still Give Better Milk, p. 151

75 ", p. 15.

76 ", p. 22-24

77 Covey, M. R. S, (2006), The Speed of Trust, p. 41 – 135

78 Conners, R & Smith T (2012), Change the Culture, Change the Game, p. 127

79 Gordon, A. S. (2021). UNBIAS, Addressing Unconscious Bias at Work – introduction – p. 2

80 "– p. 2

81 Gordon, A. S. (2021). UNBIAS, Addressing Unconscious Bias at Work

82  ". p. 6-13

83  " p. 10

84  Kee, J. E., & Newcomer, K. E. (2008). Why do change efforts fail? Public
    Manager, 37(3), 5-12

85  ", p. 5-12.

86  Catlette, B. & Hadden R. (2012). Contented Cows Still Give Better Milk, p. 40
    Conners, R & Smith T (2012), Change the Culture, Change the Game, p. 85
    Watkins, Michael. 2003. The First 90 Days. Boston, MA: Harvard Business
    Review Press.

# References Reviewed and Cited

Bradberry, T., & Greaves, J. (2005). The Emotional Intelligence Quick Book: Everything you need to know to put your Eq to work. (book) Simon & Schuster.

Bustin, G (2014). Accountability: The key to driving a high-performance culture. McGraw-Hill.

Catlette, B. & Hadden R. (2012). Contented Cows Still Give Better Milk" The Plain Truth About Employee Engagement and your Bottom Line, Revised and Expanded. (book) Wiley.

Cochran, T (2015). From Rules to Results – A Guide to Public Service Performance Transition

Collins, J. (2001). Level 5 Leadership: the triumph of humility and fierce resolve. Harvard Business Review. 83(7/8), 136-146.

Conners, R & Smith T (2012), Change the Culture, Change the Game: The Breakthrough Strategy for Energizing Your Organization and Creating Accountability for Results, (book) Penguin Publications

Conners, R, Smith T, & Hickman C, (2010) The Oz Principle, getting results through individual and organizational accountability Revised, (book), Portfolio Publisher

Covey, S. M. R. (2008). Speed of trust. (book) Simon & Schuster.

de Waal, A. & Counet, H. (2009). Lessons learned from performance management systems implementations. International Journal of Productivity and Performance Management, 58(4), 367–390.

Dull, M. (2009). Results-Model Reform Leadership: Questions of Credible Commitment. Journal of Public Administration Research & Theory, 19(2), 255-284.

Erwin, D., & Garman, A. (2010). Resistance to organizational change: Linking research and practice. Learning & Organizational Development Journal, 31 (1), 39-56.

Frei, Frances X., and Anne Morriss. (2020) Unleashed: The Unapologetic Leader's Guide to Empowering Everyone Around You. Boston: Harvard Business Review Press.

Friedman, M. (2005). Trying hard is not good enough. How to produce measurable improvements for customers and communities. North Charleston, SC: BookSurge Publishing.

Goh, S. C. (2012). Making performance measurement systems more effective in public sector organizations. Measuring Business Excellence, 16(1), 31-42.

Gordon, A. S. (2021). UNBIAS, Addressing Unconscious Bias at Work. Wiley. New Jersey.

Hatton, J., Schroeder, K. (2007). Results-based management: friend or foe?. Development in Practice, 17(3), 426-432.

Heath, C., & Heath, D. (2007). Made to stick: Why some ideas survive, and others die. New York: (book) Random House.

Huey, L., & Ahmad, B. (2009). The moderating effects of organizational culture on the relationships between leadership behaviour and organizational commitment and between organizational commitment and job satisfaction and performance. Leadership & Organization Development Journal, 30(1), 53 - 86.

Ika, L. A., & Lytvynov, V. (2009). RBM: A shift to managing development project objectives. JGBA oct. 2009 Vol1, no.1; 55 - 76. Journal of Global Business Administration, 1(1)

Kotter, J. P. (1996) Leading Change. Boston: (book) Harvard Business School Press.

Kotter, J. P. (1995). Leading change: why Transformation efforts fail. Harvard Business Review. 73(2), 59-67.

Kotter, J. P. (2008). Developing a change-friendly culture: an interview with John P. Kotter. Leader to Leader 48. 33-38.

Kouzes, J., & Posner, B. (2008). The leadership challenge, fourth edition. [Book].

Ledimo, O. (2014). An exploratory study of transformational leadership and organizational culture in a public service organization. European Conference on Management, Leadership & Governance. 434-441.

McDavid, Jim. (2014, June 26). Have we built a system that contains a paradox? Canadian Government Executive, (20)6.

Mayne, J. (2007c). Best practices in results-based management: A review of experience. A Report for the United Nations Secretariat. New York: UN Secretariat.

Mayne, J. (2009). Building an evaluative culture: The key to effective evaluation and results management. The Canadian Journal of Program Evaluation, 24(2), 1.

Mayne, J. (2007). Challenges and lessons in implementing results-based management. Evaluation, 13(1), 87–109.

Moynihan, D. P., Pandey, S. K., & Wright, B. E. (2012). Setting the table: How transformational leadership fosters performance information use. Journal of Public Administration Research & Theory, 22(1), 143-164.

Nielsen, S. B., & Hunter, D. E. K. (2013). Challenges to and forms of complementarily between performance management and evaluation. New Directions for Evaluation. 2013(137), 115–123.

Orey, M. (2011). Results based leadership. Industrial and Commercial Training, 43(3), 146–150.

Paarlberg, L. E. & Lavigna, B. (2010), Transformational Leadership and Public Service Motivation: Driving Individual and Organizational Performance. Public Administration Review, 70 (5), 710–718.

Padovani, E., Yetano, A., & Orelli, R. L. (2010). Municipal performance measurement and management in practice: Which factors matter? Public Administration Quarterly, 34(4), 591-635.

Paul, R., & Elder, L. (2012). Critical thinking: Tools for taking charge of your learning and your life. (book). FT Press.

Power, T. (2008). Power's Case Study Analysis and Writers' Handbook. Toronto: Nelson

Rath, T. (2007). Strengths finder 2.0. New York: (book) Gallup Press.

Results-Based Management Tools at CIDA: A How-to Guide. (2013). The Government of Canada, Foreign Affairs, Trade and Development Canada.

Results based management. (2014). The United Nations University. UNU-INEWH's working manual, 2nd edition.

Sanger, M. B. (2008). Getting to the roots of change: Performance management and organizational culture. Public Performance & Management Review, 31(4), 621-653.

Sanger, M. B. (2008). From measurement to management: Breaking through the barriers to state and local performance. Public Administration Review, S70-S85.

Sanger, M. B. (2013), Does Measuring Performance Lead to Better Performance?. Journal of Policy Analysis Management, 32(1), 185–203. doi:10.1002/pam.21657

Schell, S. (2012). Measuring value in the public sector. Summit, 14(4), 1-5.

Stewart, A. (2013, April 02). Results-based management: An endangered species?. Canadian Government Executive, (19)3.

Swiss, J. (2005). A framework for assessing incentives in results-based management. Public Administration Review. 65(5). 592-602.

The Art of Focused Conversation 100 Ways to Access Group Wisdom in the Workplace (2013). (book) New Society Publishers.

The United Nations University. (2014). Results based management. UNU-INEWH's working manual, 2nd edition.

Thompson, A., Strickland, A., & Gamble, J. (2012). Crafting & Executing Strategy: The quest for competitive advantage: concepts and cases (18th ed.). New York: McGraw-Hill Irwin.

Try, D. (2008). Mind the gap, please. International Journal of Productivity and Performance Management, 57(1), 22-36.

United Nations Development Group. (2010). Results-based management handbook.

Watkins, Michael. 2003. The First 90 Days. Boston, MA: Harvard Business Review Press (book).

Wimbush, E. (2011). Implementing an outcomes approach to public management and accountability in the UK—are we learning the lessons?. Public Money & Management, 31(3).

Printed in the United States
by Baker & Taylor Publisher Services